Edward Earl of Clarendon

**Characters of eminent men in the reigns of Charles I and II**

Including the rebellion

Edward Earl of Clarendon

**Characters of eminent men in the reigns of Charles I and II**
*Including the rebellion*

ISBN/EAN: 9783337204310

Printed in Europe, USA, Canada, Australia, Japan

Cover: Foto ©ninafisch / pixelio.de

More available books at **www.hansebooks.com**

"Lord Clarendon particularly excels in characters,
"which if drawn with precision and elegance are
"as difficult to the writers, as they are agreeable
"to the readers of history. He is, in this parti-
"cular, as unrivalled among the moderns as
"Tacitus is among the ancients. They both
"saw those nice distinctions, and specific dif-
"ferences in human nature which are visible
"only to the sagacious. He paints himself in
"drawing the characters of others, and we every
"where see the clear and exact comprehension,
"the uncommon learning, the dignity, and equity
"of the Lord Chancellor in his character as a
"writer. *Granger's biog. hist.*

# CHARACTERS

OF

# EMINENT MEN

IN THE REIGNS OF

## CHARLES I. AND II.

### Including the Rebellion,

FROM THE WORKS OF

## LORD CHANCELLOR CLARENDON.

---

LONDON:

PRINTED FOR R. FAULDER, BOND-STREET.

MDCCXCIII.

## ADVERTISEMENT.

*T*HE design of this publication is to present to the reader such parts of the history of the rebellion, and the subsequent æra from the restoration to the banishment of the noble author in 1667, as develop the principles and conduct of the parties concerned.

It is to be lamented, that more attention was not paid to chronological order in the original work, where, besides an almost total deficiency of dates, the chief personages are frequently described, both at the time when they became conspicuous in public life, and at their deaths. In the arrangement of this selection, the former period is generally adopted; and, although the editor, in combining the different parts, has taken the liberty to retrench some passages which appeared to him redundant, yet he has scrupulously avoided making any alteration in the language of his author, because, as an eminent writer * has observed, ' it is characteristical of the age in which he wrote; and when the language is changed, we are not sure the sense is the same.'

To the present age, it is presumed, this volume may afford an instructive lesson, in disclosing the ambitious views of the principal actors at a time when this country was involved in all the horrors of civil war, resembling those

* Boswell's Johnson. 4to. II. 514.

*which so lately have laid waste the kingdom of France, and disturbed the peace of the nations of Europe: and as similar causes must produce similar effects, it no less becomes our duty, than our interest, to guard against the visionary projects of those who, in their endeavours to reform the English constitution, would endanger those substantial blessings which were secured to us, not by the fury of the times of Charles the first; but at the peaceable and glorious revolution in* 1688.

E. T.

---

*\** A few copies are printed in 4to. as an Appendage to the Memoirs de Grammont; or for the convenience of those who may wish to embellish them with engraved portraits, of which above an hundred may be found in Bromley's catalogue.

# CONTENTS.

|  | page |
|---|---|
| INTRODUCTION, (state of Europe in 1639), | 13 to 15 |
| Charles I. and his minister Buckingham, | 16- 22 |
| View of the Court after Buckingham's death, | 23- 43 |
| Projectors of Ship-money, | 44- 47 |
| Committee of State to reduce the Scots, in 1640, | 49- 58 |
| Speakers of the house of Commons in 1640, | 58- 62 |
| Reformers in the House of Peers, in 1640, | 62- 70 |
| ———— in the House of Commons, | 70- 78 |
| Libellers, (Prynne, &c.) | 78- 81 |
| Law officers appointed in 1640, | 81- 84 |
| New council in 1641, &c. | 84- 94 |
| Persons slain at Edge-hill, Litchfield, &c. | 95-100 |
| Privy-counsellors with the King at Oxford, | 101-113 |
| ———————— who acted with the Parliament, | 114-120 |
| Persons slain at Lansdown, Bristol, &c. | 121-126 |
| Officers with whom the King consulted in 1644, | 127-132 |
| Governors of Forts and Towns, | 133-135 |
| Persons slain, beheaded, &c. to the death of Cromwell | 137-161 |
| Illustrious persons at the Restoration, | 161-174 |
| Lord Clarendon's relations and early acquaintance, | 174-187 |
| ———————— more intimate friends, concluding with his own character, | 188-201 |
| INDEX, | 202 |

The Roman Numerals at the end of each Character refer to the History of the Rebellion in octavo; and *Life* to the octavo edition of the Life and Continuation, in three volumes.

———

In note, p. 47. dele *Porcius.*——p. 79. John Bastwick died 1654.——page 92. Archbishop Williams died 1650.

# INTRODUCTION.

About the year 1639, when England enjoyed the greatest measure of felicity that it had ever known; the two crowns of France and Spain worrying each other, by their mutual incursions and invasions, whilst they had both a civil war in their own bowels; the former, by frequent rebellions from their own factions and animosities; the latter, by the defection of Portugal; and both laboured more to ransack and burn each others dominions, than to extinguish their own fire: all Germany weltering in its own blood; and contributing to each others destruction, that the poor crown of Sweden might grow great out of their ruins, and at their charge: Denmark and Poland being adventurers in the same destructive enterprizes: Holland and the United Provinces, wearied and tired with their long and chargeable war, how prosperous soever they were in it; and beginning to be more afraid of France, their ally, than of Spain their enemy: Italy every year infested by the arms of Spain and France, which divided the princes thereof into the several factions.

Of all the princes of Europe, the King of England alone seemed to be seated upon that pleasant promontory, that might safely view the tragic sufferings of all his neighbours about him, without any other concernment, than what arose from his own princely heart and christian compassion, to see such desolation wrought by the pride, and passion, and ambition, of private persons, supported by princes, who knew not what themselves would have. His three kingdoms flourishing in entire peace, and universal plenty; in danger of nothing but their own surfeits; and his dominions every day enlarged, by sending out colonies upon large and fruitful plantations; his strong fleets commanding all seas, and the numerous shipping of the nation bringing the trade of the world into his ports; nor could it with unquestionable security be carried any where else.

*O fortunati nimium, bona si sua nôrint!*

In this blessed conjuncture, when no other prince thought he wanted any thing to compass what he most desired to be possessed of, but the affection and friendship of the King of England: a small, scarce discernible cloud, arose in the north, which was shortly after attended with such a storm, that never gave over raging, till it had shaken, and even rooted up, the greatest and tallest cedars of the three nations; blasted all its beauty and fruitfulness, brought its strength to decay, and its glory to reproach, and almost to desolation; by such a career and deluge of wickedness and rebellion, as by not being enough foreseen, or in truth suspected, could not be prevented. I. 74. Life I. 70.

# CHARACTERS.

### CHARLES I.—BEHEADED MDCXLVIII.

TO speak first of his private qualifications as a man, before the mention of his princely and royal virtues; he was, if ever any, the most worthy of the title of an honest man; so great a lover of justice, that no temptation could dispose him to a wrongful action, except it was so disguised to him that he believed it to be just. He had a tenderness and compassion of nature, which restrained him from ever doing a hard hearted thing: and therefore he was so apt to grant pardon to malefactors, that the judges of the land represented to him the damage and insecurity to the public, that flowed from such his indulgence. And then he restrained himself from pardoning either murders, or highway robberies, and quickly discerned the fruits of his severity by a wonderful reformation of those enormities. He was very punctual and regular in his devotions; he was never known to enter upon his recreations or sports, though ever so early in the morning, before he had been at public prayers; so that on hunting days his chaplains were bound to a very early attendance. He was likewise very strict in observing the hours of his private cabinet devotion; and was so severe an exactor of gravity and reverence in all mention of religion, that he could never endure any light or profane word, with what sharpness of wit soever it was covered: and though he was well pleased, and delighted with reading verses made upon any occasion, no man durst bring before him any thing that was profane or unclean. That kind of wit had never any countenance then. He was so great an example of conjugal affection, that they who did not imitate him in that particular, durst not brag of their liberty: and he did not only permit, but direct his bishops, to prosecute those scandalous vices, in the ecclesiastical courts, against persons of eminence, and near relation to his service.

His kingly virtues had some mixture and alloy, that hindered them from shining in full lustre, and from producing those fruits they should have been attended with. He was not in his nature very bountiful, though he gave very much. This appeared more after the Duke of Buckingham's death, after which those showers fell very rarely; and he paused too long in giving, which made those to whom he gave, less sensible of the benefit. He kept state to the full, which made his court very orderly; no man presuming to be seen in a place where he had no pretence to be. He saw, and observed men long, before he received them about his person; and did not love strangers, nor very confident men. He was a patient hearer of causes; which he frequently accustomed himself to, at the council board; and judged very well, and was dexterous in the mediating part: so that he often put an end to causes by persuasion, which the stubborness of men's humours made dilatory in courts of justice.

He was very fearless in his person; but, in his riper years, not very enterprizing. He had an excellent understanding, but was not confident enough of it; which made him oftentimes change his own opinion for a worse, and follow the advice of men that did not judge so well as himself. This made him more irresolute than the conjuncture of his affairs would admit: if he had been of a rougher and more imperious nature, he would have found more respect and duty. And his not applying some severe cures to approaching evils, proceeded from the lenity of his nature, and the tenderness of his conscience, which, in all cases of blood made him choose the softer way, and not hearken to severe counsels, how reasonably soever urged. This only, restrained him from pursuing his advantage in the first Scottish expedition, when, humanly speaking, he might have reduced that nation to the most entire obedience that could have been wished. After all this, a man might reasonably believe that nothing less than an universal defection of three nations could have reduced a great king to so hard a fate; it is most certain, that, in that very hour when he was wickedly murdered in the sight of the sun, he had as great a share in the hearts and affections of his subjects in general, was as much beloved, esteemed, and longed for by the people in general of the three nations as any of his predecessors had ever been.

To conclude, he was the worthiest gentleman, the best master, the best friend, the best husband, the best father, and the best Christian, that the age in which he lived produced. And if he were not the greatest king, if he were without some parts and qualities which have made some kings great and happy, no other prince was ever unhappy who was possessed of half his virtues and endowments, and so much without any kind of vice. III. 256.

---

GEORGE VILLIERS; CR. DUKE OF BUCKINGHAM, THE FAVOURITE OF JAMES AND CHARLES I.—STABBED BY FELTON, MDCXXVIII.

THIS great man was a person of a noble nature, and generous disposition, and of such other endowments, as made him very capable of being a great favourite to a great king. He understood the arts of a court, and all the learning that is professed there, exactly well. By long practice in business under a master that discoursed excellently, and surely knew all things wonderfully, and took much delight in indoctrinating his young unexperienced favourite, who, he knew, would be always looked upon as the workmanship of his own hands, he had obtained a quick conception, and apprehension of business, and had the habit of speaking very gracefully, and pertinently. He was of a most flowing courtesy and affability to all men who made any address to him; and so desirous to oblige them, that he did not enough consider the value of the obligation, or the merit of the person he chose to oblige; from which, much of his misfortune resulted. He was of a courage not to be daunted, which was manifested in all his actions, and in his contests with particular persons of the greatest reputation; and especially in his whole demeanour at the isle of Rhee, both at the landing, and upon the retreat; in both which no man was more fearless, or more ready to expose himself to the highest dangers. His kindness and affection to his friends was so vehement, that they were as so many marriages for better and worse, and so many leagues offensive and defensive; as if he thought himself obliged to love all his friends, and to make war upon all they were angry with, let the cause be what it would. And it cannot be denied, that he was an enemy in the same excess; and prosecuted those he looked upon as his enemies, with the utmost rigour and animosity; and was not easily induced to reconciliation.

His single misfortune was (which indeed was productive of many greater) that he never made a noble and a worthy friendship with a man so near his equal, that he would frankly advise him for his honour, and true interest, against the current, or rather the torrent of his impetuous passions. It may reasonably be believed, that if he had been blessed with one faithful friend, who had been qualified with wisdom and integrity, that great person would have committed as few faults, and done as transcendent worthy actions, as any man who shined in such a sphere in that age in Europe. For he was of an excellent disposition, and of a mind very capable of advice and counsel. He was in his nature just and candid, liberal, generous, and bountiful; nor was it ever known, that the temptation of money swayed him to do an unjust, or unkind thing.

If he had an immoderate ambition, with which he was charged, it doth not appear that it was in his nature, or that he brought it with him to the court, but rather found it there. I. 31.

### SIR THOMAS COVENTRY, LORD KEEPER OF THE GREAT SEAL; CR. LORD COVENTRY——DIED MDCXXXIX.

HE was Recorder of London, Solicitor General, and King's Attorney before he was forty years of age; a rare ascent! all which offices he discharged with great abilities, and singular reputation of integrity. He enjoyed the place of Keeper of the Great Seal with universal reputation (and sure justice was never better administered) for the space of about sixteen years even to his death, which was another important circumstance of his felicity; that great office being so slippery, that no man had died in it before, for near the space of forty years; nor had his successors some time after him much better fortune.

He was a man of wonderful gravity and wisdom; and understood not only the whole science and mystery of the law, at least equally with any man who had ever sat in that place; but had a clear conception of the whole policy of the government both of church and state, which, by the unskilfulness of some well-meaning men, justled each the other too much.

He knew the temper, disposition, and genius of the kingdom most exactly; saw their spirits grow every day more sturdy, inquisitive, and impatient: and therefore naturally abhorred all innovations, which, he foresaw, would produce ruinous effects. Yet many, who stood at a distance, thought he was not active, and stout enough in opposing those innovations. For though, by his place, he presided in all public councils, and was most sharp-sighted in the consequence of things; yet he was seldom known to speak in matters of state, which he well knew were, for the most part, concluded, before they were brought to that public agitation; never, in foreign affairs, which the vigour of his judgment could well have comprehended: nor indeed freely in any thing, but what immediately, and plainly concerned the justice of the kingdom; and in that, as much as he could, he procured references to the judges. Though, in his nature, he had not only a firm gravity, but a severity, and even some morosity; yet it was so happily tempered, and his courtesy, and affability towards all men so transcendent, and so much without affectation, that it marvelously recommended him to all men of all degrees, and he was looked upon as an excellent courtier, without receding from the native simplicity of his own manners.

He had, in the plain way of speaking and delivery, without much ornament of elocution, a strange power of making himself believed: the only justifiable design of eloquence. He died in a season most opportune, in which a wise man would have prayed to have finished his course, and which, in truth, crowned his other signal prosperity in the world. I. 45. 131.

---

SIR RICHARD WESTON; CR. EARL OF PORTLAND, LORD HIGH TREASURER—DIED MDCXXXIV.

HE was a gentleman of a very ancient extraction by father and mother. His education had been very good amongst books and men. After some years study of the law, in the Middle Temple, he travelled into foreign parts, and at an age fit to make observations, and reflections; out of which that, which is commonly called experience, is constituted. After this he betook himself to the court, and lived there some years; at that distance, and with that awe, as was agreeable to the modesty of the age, when men were seen some time, before they were known; and well known, before they were preferred, or durst pretend to it. He took more pains in examining and inquiring into other men's offices, than in the discharge of his own; and not so much joy in what he had, as trouble and agony for what he had not. The truth is, he had so vehement a desire to be the sole favourite, that he had no relish of the power he had: and in that contention he had many rivals, who had credit enough to do him ill offices, though not enough to satisfy their own ambition; the king himself being resolved to hold the reins in his own hands, and to put no further trust in others, than was necessary for the capacity they served in. Which resolution in his majesty was no sooner believed, and the Treasurer's pretence taken notice of, than he found the number of his enemies exceedingly increased, and others to be less eager in the pursuit of his friendship; and every day discovered some infirmities in him, which being before known to few, and not taken notice of, did now expose him both to public reproach, and to private animosities: and even his vices admitted those contradictions in them, that he could hardly enjoy the pleasant fruit of any of them.

He quickly lost the character of a bold, stout, and magnanimous man, which he had been long reputed to be, in worse times; and in his most prosperous season, fell under the reproach of being a man of big looks, and of a mean and abject spirit.

To conclude, all the honours the king conferred upon him (as he made him a Baron, then an Earl, and Knight of the Garter; and above this, gave a young beautiful lady, nearly allied to his majesty,* and to the crown of Scotland, in marriage to his eldest son) could not make him think himself great enough. Nor could all the king's bounties, nor his own large accessions, raise a fortune to his heir; but after six or eight years spent in outward opulency, and inward murmur and trouble that it was not greater; after vast sums of money and great wealth gotten, and rather consumed than enjoyed; without any sense or delight in so great prosperity, with the agony that it was no greater; he died unlamented by any; bitterly mentioned by most who never pretended to love him; and severely censured, and complained of by those who expected most

* A daughter of Esme Stuart, Duke of Lenox.

from him, and deserved best of him; and left a numerous family, which was in a short time worn out, and yet outlived the fortune he left behind him.* I. 47.

---

SIR HENRY MONTAGU,† LORD PRIVY SEAL, CR. EARL OF MANCHESTER.—DIED MDCXLII.

HE was a man of great industry, and sagacity in business, which he delighted in exceedingly;

* The following is the substance of a ridiculous story respecting him.—The Earl of Tullibardine, with the Treasurer's permission, gave him a memorandum of a promise to Sir Julius Cæsar: some days after, the Treasurer found this paper, of which he had no recollection, and in which was only written "remember Cæsar." After a serious deliberation with his friends, the paper was supposed to be an intimation of a conspiracy against his life; he accordingly kept himself at home, and refused admission to any but known friends; till, on the Earl of Tullibardine's again asking him "if he had remembered Cæsar," the Treasurer recollected the ground of his perturbation. I. 52.

† He had been Lord Chief Justice of the King's Bench, and Lord High Treasurer: and was created Viscount Mandeville in the reign of James I.

and preserved so great a vigour of mind, even to his death (when he was very near eighty years of age) that some, who had known him in his younger years, did believe him to have much quicker parts in his age, than before. His honours had grown faster upon him than his fortunes, which made him too solicitous to advance the latter, by all the ways which offered themselves; whereby he exposed himself to some inconvenience, and many reproaches, and became less capable of serving the public by his counsels, and authority; which his known wisdom, long experience, and confessed gravity, and ability, would have enabled him to have done; most men considering more the person that speaks, than the things he says. And he was unhappily too much used as a check upon the lord Coventry; and when that lord perplexed their counsels and designs, with inconvenient objections in law, the authority of the lord Manchester, who had trod the same paths, was still called upon; and he did too frequently gratify their unjustifiable designs and pretences: a guilt and mischief, all men who are obnoxious, or who are thought to be so, are liable to, and can hardly preserve themselves from. But his virtues so far weighed down his infirmities, that he maintained a good general reputation and credit with the whole nation, and people; he being always looked upon, as full of integrity, and zeal to the protestant religion, as it was established by law, and of unquestionable loyalty, duty, and fidelity to the king; which two qualifications will ever gather popular breath enough to fill the sails, if the vessel be competently provided with ballast. He died in a lucky time, in the beginning of the rebellion, when neither religion, loyalty, law, nor wisdom, could have provided for any man's security. I. 54.

---

THOMAS HOWARD, EARL OF ARUNDEL; EARL MARSHAL OF ENGLAND—DIED MDCXLVI.

WAS the next officer of state who, in his own right, and quality, preceded the rest of the council. He was generally thought to be a proud man, who lived always within himself, and to himself, conversing little with any who were in common conversation; so that he seemed to live, as it were, in another nation, his house being a place to which all people resorted who resorted to no other place; strangers, or such who affected to look like strangers, and dressed themselves accordingly. He resorted sometimes to the court, because there only, was a greater man than himself; and went thither the seldomer, because there was a greater man than himself. He lived towards all favourites, and great officers, without any kind of condescension, and rather suffered himself to be ill treated by their power and authority (for he was often in disgrace, and once or twice prisoner in the tower) than to descend in making any application to them. He was willing to be thought a scholar, and to understand the most mysterious parts of antiquity, because he made a wonderful and costly purchase of excellent statues, whilst he was in Italy and in Rome (some whereof he could never obtain permission to remove from Rome, though he had paid for them) and had a rare collection of the most curious medals. As to all parts of learning he was almost illiterate, and thought no other part of history so considerable, as what related to his own family; in which, no doubt, there had been some very memorable persons. It cannot be denied that he had in his person, in his aspect, and countenance, the appearance of a great man, which he preserved in his gait and motion. He wore and affected a habit very different from that of the time, such as men had only beheld in the pictures of the most considerable men; all which drew the eyes of most, and the reverence of many towards him, as the image and representative of the primitive nobility, and native gravity of the nobles, when they had been most venerable: but this was only his outside; his nature and true humour being much disposed to levity and delights, which indeed were very despicable and childish.

He was rather thought not to be much concerned for religion, than to incline to this or that party of any: and had little other affection for the nation or the kingdom, than as he had a great share in it, in which, like the great leviathan, he might sport himself; from which he withdrew, as soon as he discerned the repose thereof was like to be disturbed, and died in Italy, under the same doubtful character of religion in which he lived. I. 55.

## WILLIAM HERBERT, THIRD EARL OF PEMBROKE, LORD CHAMBERLAIN OF THE HOUSEHOLD—DIED MDCXXX.

HE was very well bred, and of excellent parts, and a graceful speaker upon any subject, having a good proportion of learning, and a ready wit to apply it, and enlarge upon it: of a pleasant and facetious humour, and a disposition affable, generous, and magnificent.

After the fall of the Earl of Somerset, he was made lord chamberlain of the king's house, more for the court's sake, than his own; and the court appeared with the more lustre, because he had the government of that province. As he spent and lived upon his own fortune, so he stood upon his own feet, without any other support than of his proper virtue and merit; and lived towards the favourites with that decency, as would not suffer them to censure or reproach his master's judgment, and election, but as with men of his own rank. He was exceedingly beloved in the court, because he never desired to get that for himself which others laboured for, but was still ready to promote the pretences of worthy men. And he was equally celebrated in the country, for having received no obligations from the court, which might corrupt or sway his affections and judgment: so that all who were displeased, and unsatisfied in the court, or with the court, were always inclined to put themselves under his banner, if he would have admitted them; and yet he did not so reject them, as to make them choose another shelter; but so far suffered them to depend on him, that he could restrain them from breaking out beyond private resentments and murmurs.

He was a great lover of his country, and of the religion and justice, which he believed could only support it; and his friendships were only with men of those principles. And as his conversation was most with men of the most pregnant parts, and understanding, so towards any such, who needed support, or encouragement, though unknown, if fairly recommended to him, he was very liberal. Sure never man was planted in a court that was fitter for that soil, or brought better qualities with him to purify that air! Yet his memory must not be flattered, that his virtues and good inclinations may be believed; he was not without some alloy of vice, and without being clouded with great infirmities, which he had in too exorbitant a proportion. He indulged to himself pleasures of all kinds, almost in all excesses.

He died exceedingly lamented by men of all qualities, and left many of his servants and dependants owners of good estates, raised out of his employments, and bounty. I. 56.

---

### PHILIP HERBERT, CR. EARL OF MONTGOMERY; FOURTH EARL OF PEMBROKE, AND LORD CHAMBERLAIN OF THE HOUSEHOLD——DIED MDCXLIX.

BEING a young man, scarce of age at the entrance of king James, had the good fortune by the comeliness of his person, his skill, and indefatigable industry in hunting, to be the first who drew the king's eyes towards him with affection; which was quickly so far improved, that he had the reputation of a favourite. Before the end of the first, or second year, he was made gentleman of the king's bed-chamber, and earl of Montgomery; which did the king no harm: for besides that he received the king's bounty with more moderation than other men, who succeeded him; he was generally known, and as generally esteemed; being the son of one earl of Pembroke, and younger brother to another, who liberally supplied his expence, beyond what his annuity from his father would bear. Yet as neither his nature, nor his parts were improvable, so they were liable to be corrupted by any assaults; his understanding being easy to be imposed upon, and his nature being made up of very strong passions. Whilst there was tranquillity in the kingdom, he enjoyed his full share in pomp and greatness; the largeness and plentifulness of his fortune being attended with reverence and dependence from the people where his estate and interest lay, and where indeed he was a great man; getting an affection and esteem from persons who had no dependence upon him, by his magnificent living, and discoursing highly of justice, and of the protestant religion; inveighing bitterly against popery, and telling what he used to say to the king; and speaking frankly of the oversights of the court, that he might not be thought a slave to it. He had been bred from his cradle in the court; and had that perfection of a courtier, that, as he was not wary enough in offending men, so he was forward in acknowledging it, even to his inferiors, and to impute it to his passion, and ask pardon for it; which made him be thought a well natured man. Besides, he had an office, which entitled him to the exercise of some rudeness, and the good order of the court had some dependence upon his incivilities. I. 59. II. 207.

---

EDWARD SACKVILLE, FOURTH EARL OF DORSET, LORD CHAMBERLAIN TO THE QUEEN—DIED MDCLII.

HIS person was beautiful, graceful, and vigorous; his wit pleasant, sparkling, and sublime; and his other parts of learning, and language, of that lustre, that he could not miscarry in the world. The vices he had, were of the age, which he was not stubborn enough to contemn, or resist. He was a younger brother, and grandchild to the great treasurer Buckhurst, created, at the king's first entrance, earl of Dorset (he inherited the title from his brother, without much to support it) which exposed him to many difficulties, and inconveniences.

Yet his known great parts, and the very general reputation he had acquired, notwithstanding his defects (for as he was eminent in the house of commons, whilst he sat there, so he shined in the house of peers, when he came to move in that sphere) inclined king James to call him to his privy-council before his death, and if he had not too much cherished his natural constitution and propensity, he would have been an excellent man of business; for he had a very sharp discerning spirit, and was a man of an obliging nature, much honour, and great generosity, and of most entire fidelity to the crown. I. 59.

---

**JAMES HAY, CR. EARL OF CARLISLE————DIED MDCXXXVI.**

HE was surely a man of the greatest expence in his own person, of any in the age he lived; and introduced more of that expence in the excess of clothes and diet than any other man; and was indeed the original of all those inventions, from which others did but transcribe copies. He had a great universal understanding, and could have taken as much delight in any other way, if he had thought any other as pleasant, and worth his care. But he found business was attended with more rivals, and vexations; and, he thought, with much less pleasure, and not more innocence.

. He left behind him the reputation of a very fine gentleman, and a most accomplished courtier; and, after having spent, in a very jovial life, above four hundred thousand pounds, which, upon a strict computation, he received from the crown, he left not a house, nor acre of land to be remembered by. And when he had in his prospect (for he was very sharp sighted, and saw as far before him as most men) the gathering together of that cloud in Scotland, which shortly after covered both kingdoms, he died with as much tranquillity of mind, to all appearance, as used to attend a man of more severe exercise of virtue; and with as little apprehension of death, which he expected many days. I. 62.

HENRY RICH, CR. EARL OF HOLLAND, YOUNGER BROTHER OF THE EARL OF WARWICK—BEHEADED MDCXLVIII.

HE was a very handsome man, of a lovely and winning presence, and genteel conversation, by which he got so easy an admission into the court and grace of king James, that he gave over the thought of further intending the life of a soldier. He took more care to be thought a good friend to parliaments, than a good servant to his master, and was thought to say too little of his having failed so much in his duty to him, which most good men believed to be the source from whence his calamity sprung.

He too much desired to enjoy ease and plenty, when the king could have neither; and did think poverty the most insupportable evil that could befal any man in the world. I. 62. III. 271.

### SIR JOHN COKE, SECRETARY OF STATE——DIED MDCXLIV.

HE was a man of a very narrow education, and a narrower nature; having continued long in the university of Cambridge,* where he had gotten Latin learning enough; and afterwards in the country in the condition of a private gentleman, till after he was fifty years of age; when, upon some reputation he had for industry and diligence, he was called to some painful employment in the office of the navy, which he discharged well; and afterwards to be master of requests, and then to be secretary of state; which he enjoyed to a great age: and was a man rather unadorned with any parts of vigour and quickness, and unendowed with any notable virtues, than notorious for any weakness or defect of understanding, or transported with any vicious inclinations, appetite to money only excepted. His cardinal perfection was industry, and his most eminent infirmity covetousness. His long experience had informed him well of the state and affairs of England; but of foreign transactions, or the common interest of christian princes, he was entirely undiscerning and ignorant. I. 64. 122.

* For which he was M. P. and a fellow of trinity college.

### SIR DUDLEY CARLETON, CR. VISCOUNT DORCHESTER; ONE OF THE PRINCIPAL SECRETARIES OF STATE—DIED MDCXXXI.

HE was of a quite contrary nature, constitution, and education,* and understood all that related to foreign employments, and the condition of other princes, and nations very well; but was unacquainted with the government, laws, and customs of his own country, and the nature of the people. He was a younger son in a good gentleman's family, and bred in Christ church, in the university of Oxford, where he was a student of the foundation, and a young man of parts, and towardly expectation.

He was twice ambassador extraordinary in Holland, and was the last who was admitted to be

---

* Compared with Sir J. Coke.

Sir Dudley Carleton lived in times, when men imagined to themselves some unknown bliss from untried governments; when public clamours were loud, and dessentions high: and by way of mitigating all such restlesness of spirit, he used frequently to say, that "There will be mistakes in divinity, while men preach, and errors in government, while men govern." *Biog. Dic.*

present, and to vote in the general assembly of the states, under that character; of which great privilege the crown had been possessed from a great part of the reign of queen Elizabeth, and through the time of king James, to that moment; which administered fresh matter of murmur for the giving up the towns of the Brill and Flushing, which had been done some years before by king James; without which men thought those states would not have had the courage so soon to have degraded the crown of England from a place in their councils, which had prospered so eminently under the shadow of that power and support. As soon as he returned from Holland, he was called to the privy-council. The making him secretary of state, and a peer of the realm, when his estate was scarce visible, was the last piece of workmanship the duke of Buckingham lived to finish, who seldom satisfied himself with conferring a single obligation. I. 64.

## WILLIAM NOY, ATTORNEY-GENERAL——DIED MDCXXXIV.

HE was by much industry and importunity from court, persuaded to accept that place, for which all other men laboured (being the best for profit that profession is capable of), and so he suffered himself to be made the king's attorney-general. The court made no impression upon his manners; upon his mind it did: and though he wore about him an affected morosity, which made him unapt to flatter other men, yet even that morosity and pride rendered him the most liable to be grossly flattered himself, that can be imagined. And by this means the great persons, who steered the public affairs, by admiring his parts, and extolling his judgment, as well to his face, as behind his back, wrought upon him by degrees, for the eminency of the service, to be an instrument in all their designs; thinking that he could not give a clearer testimony, that his knowledge in the law was greater than all other men's, than by making that law, which all other men believed not to be so. So he moulded, framed, and pursued, the odious project of soap; and with his own hand drew, and prepared the writ for ship-money;* both which will be the lasting monuments of his fame. In a word, he was an unanswerable instance, how necessary a good education, and a knowledge of men, are, to make a wise man, at least, a man fit for business. I. 73.

---

SIR JOHN FINCH, LORD CH. JUST. COMMON PLEAS; CR. LORD FINCH OF FORDWICH, LORD KEEPER —DIED IN EXILE MDCLX.

HE had much that the other † wanted, but nothing that the other had. Having led a free life, in a restrained fortune, and having set up upon the

* It was directed to the sheriff of every county in England " to provide a ship of war for the king's service, and to send " it amply provided and fitted, by such a day, to such a " place (and with that writ were sent to each sheriff instruc- " tions) that, instead of a ship, he should levy upon his county " such a sum of money, and return the same to the treasurer " of the navy, for his majesty's use." Hence the denomination of ship-money. I. 68.

† Noy.

stock of a good wit, and natural parts, without the superstructure of much knowledge in the profession by which he was to grow; he was willing to use those weapons in which he had most skill, and so (being not unseen in the affections of the court, but not having reputation enough to guide, or reform them) he took up ship-money where Mr. Noy left it; and, being a judge, carried it up to that pinnacle, from whence he almost broke his own neck; having, in his journey thither, had too much influence on his brethren to induce them to concur in a judgment they had all cause to repent.\* To which, his declaration after he was

---

\* " These men (said our author, in a speech to the lords) have, upon vulgar fears, delivered up the precious forts they were trusted with, almost without assault; and in a tame, easy trance of flattery and servitude, lost and forfeited (shamefully forfeited) that reputation, awe, and reverence, which the wisdom, courage, and gravity, of their venerable predecessors, had contracted and fastened to their places; and have even rendered that study and profession, which in all ages hath been, and I hope now shall be, of honourable estimation, so contemptible and vile, that had not this blessed day come (the day of impeachment of the six judges) all men would have had that quarrel to the law itself, which

keeper of the great seal of England, must be added, upon a demurrer put in to a bill before him, which had no other equity in it, than an order of the lords of the council; " that whilst he " was keeper, no man should be so saucy as to " dispute those orders, but that the wisdom of that " board should be always ground enough for him " to make a decree in chancery:" which was so great an aggravation of the excess of that table, that it received more prejudice from that act of unreasonable countenance and respect, than from all the contempt that could possibly have been offered to it. I. 73.

---

### GEORGE ABBOT, ARCHBISHOP OF CANTERBURY; —DIED MDCXXXIII.

HE considered the christian religion no otherwise, than as it abhorred and reviled popery, and valued those men most, who did that the most furiously.

*Marcius Porcius* had to the Greek tongue, who thought it a mockery to learn that language, the masters whereof lived in bondage under others." State Trials, I. 709. VII. 309.

For the strict observation of the discipline of the church, or the conformity to the articles, or canons established, he made little inquiry, and took less care; and having himself made a very little progress in the ancient and solid study of divinity, he adhered only to the doctrine of Calvin; and for his sake, did not think so ill of the discipline as he ought to have done. But if men prudently forbore a public reviling, and railing at the hierarchy, and ecclesiastical government, let their opinions and private practice be what they would, they were not only secure from any inquisition of his, but acceptable to him, and, at least, equally preferred by him. And though many other bishops plainly discerned the mischiefs, which daily broke in to the prejudice of religion, by his defects and remissness, and prevented it in their own diocesses as much as they could, and gave all their countenance to men of other parts, and other principles; and though the bishop of London, Dr. Laud, from the time of his authority and credit with the king, had applied all the remedies he could to those defections, and from the time of his being chancellor of Oxford, had much discountenanced, and almost suppressed that spirit, by encouraging another kind of learning and practice, in that university, which was indeed according to the doctrine of the church of England; yet that temper in the archbishop, whose house was a sanctuary to the most eminent of that factious party, and who licensed their most pernicious writings, left his successor a very difficult work to do, to reform, and reduce a church into order, that had been so long neglected, and that was so ill filled by many weak, and more wilful church-men. I. 88.

---

**WILLIAM LAUD, ARCHBISHOP OF CANTERBURY;**
**—BEHEADED MDCXLIV.**

HE was a man of great parts, and very exemplary virtues, alloyed and discredited by some unpopular, natural infirmities; the greatest of which was (besides a hasty sharp way of expressing himself) that he believed innocence of heart, and integrity of manners, was a guard strong enough to secure any man in his voyage through this world, in what company soever he travelled, and through what ways soever he was to pass: and sure never any man was better supplied with that provision. He had great courage and resolution, and being most assured within himself, that he proposed no end in all his actions and designs, but what was pious and just (as sure no man had ever a heart more entire to the king, the church, or his country), he never studied the easiest ways to those ends; he thought, it may be, that any art or industry that way, would discredit, at least make the integrity of the end suspected, let the cause be what it will. He did court persons too little; nor cared to make his designs and purposes appear as candid as they were, by shewing them in any other dress, than their own natural beauty, though perhaps in too rough a manner; and did not consider enough what men said, or were like to say of him. If the faults and vices were fit to be looked into, and discovered, let the persons be who they would that were guilty of them, they were sure to find no connivance of favour from him.

On the death of the earl of Portland (1634) he was made one of the commissioners of the treasury*

---

\* In 1640, the weight and envy of all great matters of state rested upon archbishop Laud, the earl of Strafford, and

and revenue, which he had reason to be sorry for, because it engaged him in civil business, and matters of state, wherein he had little experience, and which he had hitherto avoided.

He defended himself (on his trial) with great and undaunted courage, and less passion than was expected from his constitution; answered all their objections with clearness, and irresistible reason; and convinced all impartial men of his integrity, and his detestation of all treasonable intentions. So that though few excellent men have ever had fewer friends to their persons, yet all reasonable men absolved him from any foul crime that the law could take notice of, and punish. However, when they had said all they could against him, and he all for himself that need be said, and no such crime appearing, as the lords, as the supreme court of judicatory, would take upon them to judge him to be worthy of death; they resorted to their legislative power, and by ordinance of parliament, as they called it, that is, by a determination of those

lord Cottington, who were at the head of the then committee of state: the marquis of Hamilton, by his skill and interest, bore as great a part as he had a mind to do, and had the skill to meddle no further than he had a mind. I. 149.

members who sat in the houses (whereof in the house of peers there were not above twelve), they appointed him to be put to death, as guilty of high treason. The first time the two houses of parliament had ever assumed that jurisdiction, or that ever ordinance had been made to such a purpose; nor could any rebellion be more against law than that murderous act. He underwent his execution with all christian courage and magnanimity, to the admiration of the beholders, and confusion of his enemies. I. 90. II. 572.

---

SIR THOMAS WENTWORTH, CR. EARL OF STRAFFORD;* LORD PRESIDENT OF THE NORTH—BEHEADED MDCXLI.

HE was a man of great parts, and extraordinary endowments of nature; not unadorned with some

* And baron of Raby, a house belonging to Sir Henry Vane, and an honour he made account should belong to himself; which was an act of the most unnecessary provocation (though he contemned the man with marvellous scorn), that I have known, and I believe was the chief occasion of the loss of the earl's head. I. 150.

L<sup>d</sup> STRAFFORD

Pub June 1 1794 by I Herbert Pall Mall

addition of art and learning, though that again was more improved and illustrated by the other; for he had a readiness of conception, and sharpness of expression, which made his learning thought more than in truth it was. His first inclinations and addresses to the court, were only to establish his greatness in the country; where he apprehended some acts of power from the lord Savile, who had been his rival always there, and of late had strengthened himself by being made a privy-counsellor, and officer at court: but his first attempts were so prosperous, that he contented not himself with being secure from the lord's power in the country, but rested not till he had bereaved his adversary of all power and place in court; and so sent him down, a most abject, disconsolate old man, to his country, where he was to have the superintendancy over him too, by getting himself at that time made lord president of the north. These successes, applied to a nature too elate and haughty of itself, and a quicker progress into the greatest employments and trust, made him more transported with disdain of other men, and more contemning the forms of business, than happily he would have been, if he had met with some interruptions in the beginning, and had passed in a more leisurely gradation to the office of a statesman.

He was, no doubt, of great observation, and a piercing judgment, both in things and persons; but his too good skill in persons, made him judge the worse of things: for it was his misfortune, to be in a time wherein very few wise men were equally employed with him; and scarce any (but the lord Coventry, whose trust was more confined) whose faculties and abilities were equal to his: so that upon the matter he relied wholly upon himself; and discerning many defects in most men, he too much neglected what they said or did. Of all his passions, his pride was most predominant: which a moderate exercise of ill fortune might have corrected and reformed; and which was by the hand of heaven strangely punished, by bringing his destruction upon him, by two things that he most despised—the people and Sir Harry Vane. In a word, the epitaph which Plutarch records that Sylla wrote for himself, may not be unfitly applied to him, " That no man did ever exceed him, either " in doing good to his friends, or in doing mischief " to his enemies; for his acts of both kinds were " most notorious." I. 259.

## SIR FRANCIS COTTINGTON, CR. LORD COTTINGTON; CHANCELLOR OF THE EXCHEQUER—— DIED MDCLI.

HE was a very wise man, by the great and long experience he had in business of all kinds; and by his natural temper, which was not liable to any transport of anger, or any other passion, but could bear contradiction, and even reproach, without being moved, or put out of his way: for he was very steady in pursuing what he proposed to himself, and had a courage not to be frighted with any opposition. It is true, he was illiterate as to the grammar of any language, or the principles of any science, but by his perfectly understanding the Spanish (which he spoke as a Spaniard), the French, and Italian languages, and having read very much in all, he could not be said to be ignorant in any part of learning, divinity only excepted. He had a very fine and extraordinary understanding in the nature of beasts and birds, and above all, in all kind of plantations, and arts of husbandry.

He raised by his own virtue and industry a very fair estate, of which, though the revenue did not exceed above four thousand pounds by the year; yet he had four very good houses, and three parks, the value whereof was not reckoned into that computation.

He was of an excellent humour, and very easy to live with; and under a grave countenance, covered the most of mirth, and caused more, than any man of the most pleasant disposition. He never used any body ill, but used many very well for whom he had no regard: his greatest fault was, that he could dissemble, and make men believe that he loved them very well, when he cared not for them. He had not very tender affections, nor bowels apt to yearn at all objects which deserved compassion. He was heartily weary of the world, and no man was more willing to die; which is an argument that he had peace of conscience. He left behind him a greater esteem of his parts, than love to his person. I. 151. III. 382.

## JAMES, MARQUIS OF HAMILTON; CR. DUKE—BEHEADED MDCXLVIII.

IF he had been weighed in the scales of the people's hatred, he was at that time (1640) thought to be in greater danger than any one of the other; for he had more enemies, and fewer friends, in court or country. His interest in the king's affection was at least equal, and thought to be superior, to any man's; and he had received as invidious instances, and marks of those affections. He had more out-faced the law, in bold projects and pressures upon the people, than any other man durst have presumed to do, especially in the projects of wine and iron; about the last of which, and the most gross, he had a sharp contest with the lord Coventry (who was a good wrestler too), and at last compelled him to let it pass the seal: the entire profit of which, always reverted to himself, and to such as were his pensioners.

When he ascended the scaffold (at his execution), he complained much of " the injustice that was done him; and that he was put to death for obeying the laws of his country, which if he had

not done, he must have been put to death there.*"
He acknowledged the obligations he had to the
king, and seemed not sorry for the gratitude he
had expressed, how dear soever it cost him. His
natural darkness and reservation in his discourse,
made him to be thought a wise man, and his having been in command under the king of Sweden,
and his continual discourses of battles and fortifications, made him be thought a great soldier. And
both these mistakes, were the cause that made
him be looked upon as a worse, and more dangerous man, than in truth he deserved to be. I. 152.
III. 271.

---

JOHN GLANVILLE, SERJEANT AT LAW †——DIED
MDCLXI.

HE was very well acquainted with the proceedings in parliament, of a quick conception, and of

* In Scotland. State Trials, II. 1.
† Chosen speaker H. C. April 13, 1640.—At this time, the parliamentary hours were from eight to twelve at noon. I. 132.

S B GRANVILLE..

a ready and voluble expression, dexterous in disposing the house, and very acceptable to them. When the house was in a committee, on the king's demand in lieu of ship-money, he rose up, and in a most pathetical speech, in which he excelled, he endeavoured to persuade the house " to comply with the king's desire, for the good of the nation, and to reconcile him to parliaments for ever, which this seasonable testimony of their affections would infallibly do;" and in the warmth of his discourse, which he plainly discerned made a wonderful impression upon the house, he let fall some sharp expressions against the imposition of ship-money, and the judgment in the point, which he said plainly " was against law, if he understood what law was," (who was known to be very learned) which expression, how necessary and artificial soever, to reconcile the affections of the house to the matter in question, very much irreconciled him at court, and to those upon whom he had the greatest dependence.\* I. 137.

\* Besides several of his speeches, there were published in 1775, " Cases of controverted elections in the house of commons, in 1623 and 1624, from the MSS. of Mr. Glanville, the chairman;" to which is prefixed, an historical account of

EDWARD, SECOND VISCOUNT CONWAY; GENERAL OF HORSE—DIED MDCLV.

HE had been born a soldier in his father's garrison of the Brill, when he was governor there; and bred up, in several commands, under the particular care of the lord Vere, whose nephew he was; and though he was married young, when his father was secretary of state, there was no action of the English, either at sea or land, in which he had not a considerable command; and always preserved a more than ordinary reputation. He was of a very pleasant and inoffensive conversation, which made him generally very acceptable: so that the court being at that time full of faction, very few loving one another, or those who resorted to any who were not loved by them; he alone, was even domestic with all, and not suspected by either the lords or the ladies factions. I. 141.

the ancient right of determining cases upon controverted elections, by John Topham, Esq. of Gray's Inn, barrister at law, F. S. A. *These cases are held in high estimation by parliamentary lawyers, and election committees.*

## WILLIAM LENTHAL*—DIED MDCLXI.

BEING a lawyer of competent practice, and no ill reputation for his affection to the government, both of church and state, he was pitched upon by the king, and with very great difficulty, rather prevailed with, than persuaded, to accept the charge of speaker: and no doubt a worse could not have been deputed, of all that profession, who were then returned; for he was a man of a very narrow, timorous nature, and of no experience or conversation in the affairs of the kingdom, beyond what the very drudgery in his profession (in which all

---

* Chosen speaker H. C. Nov. 3, 1640.

When the king went into the house of commons (1642) to demand the five members, he asked the speaker, who stood below, whether any of them were in the house? the speaker falling on his knee, prudently replied: "I have, sir, neither "eyes to see, nor tongue to speak in this place, but as the "house is pleased to direct me, whose servant I am: and "I humbly ask pardon, that I cannot give any other answer "to what your majesty is pleased to demand of me." HUME.

This subject now engages the pencil of Mr. Copley, who has chosen it as a companion for his celebrated picture of lord Chatham in the house of lords.

his design was to make himself rich) engaged him in. In a word, he was in all respects very unequal to the work; and not knowing how to preserve his own dignity, or to restrain the licence and exorbitance of others, his weakness contributed as much to the growing mischiefs, as the malice of the principal contrivers. I. 171.

---

FRANCIS RUSSEL, FOURTH EARL OF BEDFORD—DIED MDCXLI.

HE was of too great and plentiful a fortune to wish a subversion of the government, and it quickly appeared, that he only intended to make himself and his friends great at court, not at all to lessen the court itself. He was of great civility, and of much more good nature than any of the other; and therefore the king resolving to do his business with that party by him, resolved to make him lord high treasurer of England; and, at his desire, intended to make Mr. Pym chancellor of the exchequer, &c. He was a wise man, and would have proposed and advised moderate courses; but was not incapable, for want of resolution, of being carried into violent ones, if his advice were not submitted to: and therefore many, who knew him well, thought his death not unseasonable, as well to his fame as his fortune; and that it rescued him as well from some possible guilt, as from those visible misfortunes, which men of all conditions have since undergone. I. 182. 254.

---

**WILLIAM FIENNES, CR. LORD VISCOUNT SAY AND SELE\*—DIED MDCLXII.**

HE was a man who had the deepest hand in the original contrivance of all the calamities which befell this unhappy kingdom, though he had not the least thought of dissolving the monarchy, and less of levelling the ranks and distinctions of men; for no man valued himself more upon his title, or had more ambition to make it greater, and to raise his fortune, which was but moderate for his title. He was of a proud, morose, and sullen nature; conversed much with books, having been bred a

---

\* Lord privy seal, 1660.

scholar, and (though nobly born) a fellow of new college in Oxford.

His parts were not quick, but so much above many of his own rank, that he had always great credit, and authority in parliament, and the more, for taking all opportunities to oppose the court. He had conversation with very few, but such who had great malignity against the church and state, and fomented their inclinations, and gave them instructions how to behave themselves with caution, and to do their business with most security; and was in truth the pilot that steered all those vessels which were freighted with sedition to destroy the government.

He found always some way to make professions of duty to the king, and made several undertakings to do great services, which he could not, or would not make good; and made haste to possess himself of any preferment he could compass, whilst his friends were content to attend a more proper conjuncture. So he got the mastership of the wards shortly after the beginning of the parliament, and was as solicitous to be treasurer, after the death of the earl of Bedford; and, if he could have satisfied his rancour in any degree against the church, he would have been ready to have carried the prerogative as high as ever it was. When he thought there was mischief enough done, he would have stopped the current, and have diverted farther fury; but he then found he had only authority and credit to do hurt, none to heal the wounds he had given; and fell into as much contempt with those whom he had led, as he was with those whom he had undone. I. 182. II. 212.

---

### EDWARD MONTAGU, SECOND EARL OF MANCHESTER*—DIED MDCLXXI.

HE was of a gentle and a generous nature, civilly bred, had reverence and affection for the person of the king, upon whom he had attended in Spain; loved his country with too unskilful a tenderness, and was of so excellent a temper and disposition, that the barbarous times, and the rough parts he was forced to act in them, did not wipe out, or much deface those marks: insomuch as he was never guilty of any rudeness towards those he was obliged to oppress, but performed always as

* Lord chamberlain, 1660

good offices towards his old friends, and all other persons, as the iniquity of the time, and the nature of the employment he was in would permit him to do, which kind of humanity could be imputed to very few.

No man was courted with more application by persons of all conditions and qualities; and his person was not less acceptable to those of steady and uncorrupted principles, than to those of depraved inclinations. And in the end, even his piety administered some excuse to him; for his father's infirmities and transgressions had so far exposed him to the inquisition of justice, that the son found it necessary to procure the assistance and protection of those, who were strong enough to violate justice itself; and so he adhered to those who were best able to defend his father's honour, and thereby to secure his own fortune; and concurred with them in their most violent designs, and gave reputation to them. And the court as unskilfully took an occasion, too soon, to make him desperate, by accusing him of high treason;[*] when

[*] With the five members of the house of commons. He was then lord Kimbolton, by which title he had been called to the house of peers in the lifetime of his father.

(though he might be guilty enough) he was, without doubt, in his intentions, at least, as innocent as any of the leading men.

It is some evidence that God Almighty saw his heart was not so malicious as the rest, that he preserved him to the end of the confusion, when he appeared as glad of the king's restoration, and had heartily wished it long before; and very few who had a hand in the contrivance of the rebellion, gave so manifest tokens of repentance as he did; and having for many years undergone the jealousy and hatred of Cromwell, as one who abominated the murder of the king, and all the barbarous proceedings against the lives of men in cold blood; the king, upon his return, received him into grace and favour, which he never after forfeited by any undutiful behaviour. I. 182. II. 211.

## ROBERT DEVEREUX, THIRD EARL OF ESSEX—DIED MDCXLVI.

THOUGH he was no good speaker in public, yet by having sat long in parliament, was so well acquainted with the order of it in very active times, that he was a better speaker there than any where else, and being always heard with attention and respect, had much authority in the debates. He was a great lover of justice, and could not have been tempted to consent to the oppression of an innocent man; but in the discerning the several species of guilt, he had no faculties or measure of judging, nor was above the temptation of general prejudice; and it may be, of particular disobligations and resentments, which proceeded from the weakness of his judgment, not the malice of his nature. He had no ambition of title, or office, or preferment; but only to be kindly looked upon, and kindly spoken to, and quietly to enjoy his own fortune: and, without doubt, no man in his nature more abhorred rebellion than he did, nor could he have been led into it by any open and transparent temptation, but by a thousand disguises and cozenages. His pride supplied his want of ambition, and he was angry to see any other man more respected than himself, because he thought he deserved it more, and did better requite it: for he was in his friendships just and constant, and would not have practised foully against those he took to be enemies. No man had credit enough with him to corrupt him in point of loyalty to the king, whilst he thought himself wise enough to know what treason was. But the new doctrine and distinction of allegiance, and of the king's power in and out of parliament, and the new notions of ordinances, were too hard for him, and did really intoxicate his understanding, and made him quit his own to follow theirs, who, he thought, wished as well, and judged better than himself. His vanity disposed him to be his excellency, and his weakness to believe that he should be the general in the houses, as well as in the field, and be able to govern their councils, and restrain their passions, as well as to fight their battles; and that by this means, he should become the preserver, and not the destroyer, of the king and kingdom. With this ill-grounded confidence, he launched out into that sea, where he met with nothing but rocks and shelves, and from whence he could never discover any safe port to harbour in. II. 208. Life III. 782.

---

### JOHN PYM—DIED MDCXLIII.

NO man had more to answer for the miseries of the kingdom, or had his hand or head deeper in their contrivance; and yet, I believe, they grew much higher even in his life, than he designed. He was a man of a private quality and condition of life, his education in the office of the exchequer, where he had been a clerk, and his parts rather acquired by industry, than supplied by nature, or adorned by art. He had been well known in former parliaments, and was one of those few who had sat in many; the long intermission of parliaments having worn out most of those who had been acquainted with the rules and orders observed in those conventions. This gave him some reputation and reverence amongst those who were but now introduced. In the short parliament he spoke much, and appeared to be the most leading man;

for besides the exact knowledge of the former, and orders of that council, which few men had, he had a very comely and grave way of expressing himself, with great volubility of words, natural and proper; and understood the temper and affections of the kingdom as well as any man; and had observed the errors and mistakes in government, and knew well how to make them appear greater than they were.

Certain it is, that his power of doing shrewd turns was extraordinary, and no less in doing good offices for particular persons: and that he did preserve many from censure, who were under the severe displeasure of the houses, and looked upon as eminent delinquents; and the quality of many of them made it believed, that he had sold that protection for valuable considerations.

He died towards the end of December, before the Scots entered; and was buried with wonderful pomp and magnificence, in that place where the bones of our English kings and princes are committed to their rest. II. 462.

## JOHN HAMPDEN—DIED MDCXLIII.

HE was a gentleman of a good extraction, and a fair fortune, who, from a life of great pleasure and licence, had on a sudden retired to extraordinary sobriety and strictness, and yet retained his usual cheerfulness and affability, which, together with the opinion of his wisdom and justice, and the courage he had shewed in opposing the ship-money, raised his reputation to a very great height, not only in Buckinghamshire, where he lived, but generally throughout the kingdom. He was not a man of many words, and rarely begun the discourse, or made the first entrance upon any business that was assumed; but a very weighty speaker; and after he had heard a full debate, and observed how the house was like to be inclined, took up the argument, and shortly, and clearly, and craftily, so stated it, that he commonly conducted it to the conclusion he desired; and if he found he could not do that, he was never without the dexterity to divert the debate to another time, and to prevent the determining any thing in the negative, which might prove inconvenient in the future.

He made so great a shew of civility, and modesty, and humility, and always of mistrusting his own judgment, and esteeming his with whom he conferred for the present, that he seemed to have no opinions or resolutions, but such as he contracted from the information and instruction he received upon the discourses of others; whom he had a wonderful art of governing, and leading into his principles and inclinations, whilst they believed that he wholly depended upon their counsel and advice. No man had ever a greater power over himself, or was less the man that he seemed to be, which shortly after appeared to every body, when he cared less to keep on the mask. He was of an industry and vigilance not to be tired out, or wearied by the most laborious; and of parts not to be imposed upon, by the most subtle or sharp; and of a personal courage equal to his best parts; so that he was an enemy not to be wished wherever he might have been made a friend, and as much to be apprehended where he was so, as any man could deserve to be: and therefore his death was no less pleasing to the one party, than it was condoled in the other. In a word, what was said of Cinna, might well be applied to him; "he had a

" head to contrive, and a tongue to persuade, and
" a hand to execute, any mischief." His death therefore seemed to be a great deliverance to the nation. I. 185. II. 265.

---

OLIVER ST. JOHN, SOLICITOR GENERAL——DIED MDCLXXIII.

HE was a lawyer of Lincoln's inn, known to be of parts and industry, but not taken notice of for practice in Westminster hall, till he argued at the exchequer chamber the case of ship-money, on the behalf of Mr. Hampden; which gave him much reputation, and called him into all courts, and to all causes, where the king's prerogative was most contested. He was a man reserved, and of a dark and clouded countenance; very proud, and conversing with very few, and those, men of his own humour and inclinations. He made good the confidence of his party, by not in the least degree abating his malignant spirit, or dissembling it; but with the same obstinacy opposed every thing which might advance the king's service, when he was his solicitor, as ever he had done before. * I. 186. 211.

---

### NATHANIEL FIENNES——DIED MDCLXIX.

HE was a man of good parts of learning, and after some years spent in new college in Oxford, of which his father had been formerly fellow, had spent his time abroad in Geneva, and amongst the cantons of Swisserland, where he improved his disinclination to the church. From his travels he returned through Scotland, when that rebellion was in the bud; and was very little known, except amongst that people, until he came into parliament, when it was quickly discovered that he was the darling of his father (the lord Say), so he was like to make good whatsoever he had for many years promised. I. 186.

* He was lord chief justice of the common pleas, in the time of the commonwealth.

## SIR HENRY VANE, THE YOUNGER—EXECUTED FOR HIGH TREASON MDCLXII.*

HE. had an unusual aspect, which, though it might naturally proceed both from his father and mother, neither of which were beautiful persons, yet made men think there was something in him extraordinary; and his whole life made good that imagination.

He was indeed a man of extraordinary parts, a pleasant wit, a great understanding, which pierced into and discerned the purposes of other men with wonderful sagacity, whilst he had himself *vultum clausum*, that no man could make a guess of what he intended. He was of a temper not to be moved, and of rare dissimulation, and could comply when it was not seasonable to contradict, without losing ground by the condescension; and if he were not superior to Mr. Hampden, he was inferior to no other man, in all mysterious artifices. There need no more be said of his ability, than that he was chosen to cozen and deceive a whole nation, which was thought to excel in craft and cunning; which

* State Trials, II. 435.

he did with notable pregnancy and dexterity, and prevailed with a people, that could not otherwise be prevailed upon than by advancing their idol presbytery, to sacrifice their peace, their interest, and their faith, to the erecting a power and authority that resolved to persecute presbytery to extirpation; and in process of time, very near brought their purpose to pass. I. 186. II. 379.

---

### DENZEL HOLLES, CR. LORD HOLLES——DIED MDCLXXIX.

HE was the younger son, and younger brother, of the earls of Clare; was as much valued and esteemed by the whole party as any man; as he deserved to be, being of more accomplished parts than any of them, and of great reputation by the part he acted against the court and the duke of Buckingham, in the parliament of the fourth year of the king (the last parliament that had been before the short one in April) and his long imprisonment, and sharp prosecution afterwards, upon that account;* of which he retained the memory with acrimony enough. But he would in no degree intermeddle in the counsel, or prosecution of the earl of Strafford (which he could not prevent) who had married his sister, by whom he had all his children, which made him a stranger to all those consultations, though it did not otherwise interrupt the friendship he had with the most violent of those prosecutors. In all other contrivances, he was in the most secret councils with those who most governed, and was respected by them, with very submiss applications, as a man of authority.† I. 188.

---

### WILLIAM PRYNNE ‡——DIED MDCLXIX.

HE was not unlearned in the profession of the law, as far as learning is acquired by the mere reading of books; but, being a person of great industry, had spent more time in reading divinity;

* State Trials, VII. 242.     † Amb. Ext. to Paris, 1663.
‡ See the trial of Prynne, Bastwick, and Burton, for a libel, State Trials, I. 481.

and which marred that divinity, in the conversation of factious and hot-headed divines: and so, by a mixture of all three, with the rudeness and arrogance of his own nature, had contracted a proud and venomous dislike to the discipline of the church of England; and so, by degrees (as the progress is very natural), an equal irreverence to the government of the state too; both which he vented in several absurd, petulant, and supercilious discourses in print. I. 200.

---

JOHN BASTWICK, M. D.—DIED ABOUT MDCL.

HE was a half-witted, crack-brained fellow, unknown to either university, or the college of physicians; but one that had spent his time abroad, between the schools and the camp (for he had been in, or passed through armies), and had gotten a doctorship, and Latin; with which, in a very flowing style, with some wit, and much malice, he inveighed against the prelates of the church in a book which he printed in Holland, and industriously dispersed in London, and throughout the kingdom; having presumed (as their modesty is always equal to their obedience) to dedicate it to the sacred majesty of the king. I. 200.

---

### HENRY BURTON, B. D.—DIED MDCXLVII.

HE had formerly a kind of relation by service to the king; having, before he took orders, waited as closet keeper, and so attended at canonical hours with the books of devotion upon his majesty, when he was prince of Wales; and a little before the death of king James took orders: and so his highness coming shortly to be king; the vapours of ambition fuming into his head that he was still to keep his place, he would not think of less than being clerk of the closet to the new king, which place his majesty conferred upon, or rather continued in, the bishop of Durham, doctor Neyl, who had long served king James there. Mr. Burton thus disappointed, and, as he called it, despoiled of his right, would not, in the greatness of his heart, sit down by the affront; but committed two or three such weak, saucy indiscretions, as caused an inhibition to be sent him, "that he should not presume to come any more to court:" and from that time he resolved to revenge himself of the bishop of Durham, upon the whole order; and so turned lecturer, and preached against them; being endued with malice and boldness, instead of learning and any tolerable parts. I. 201.

---

EDWARD LITTLETON, CR. LORD LITTLETON; LORD KEEPER———DIED MDCXLV.

HE was a man of great reputation in the profession of the law, for learning and all other advantages, which attend the most eminent men; he was of a very good extraction in Shropshire, and inherited a fair fortune and inheritance from his father; he was a handsome, and a proper man, of a very graceful presence; and notorious for courage, which, in his youth, he had manifested with his sword; he had taken great pains in the hardest and most knotty part of the law, as well as that which was more customary, and was not only very ready and expert in the books, but exceedingly versed in records, in studying and examining whereof, he had kept Mr. Selden company, with whom he had great friendship, and who had much assisted him; so that he was looked upon the best antiquary of the profession, who gave himself up to practice; and upon the mere strength of his own abilities, he had raised himself into the first rank of the practisers in the common law courts; and was chosen recorder of London before he was called to the bench, and grew presently into the highest practice in all the other courts, as well as those of the law. He was made solicitor general, much to his honour, but not to his profit; the obligation of attendance upon that office, depriving him of much benefit he used to acquire by his practice, before he had that relation. Upon the death of the lord Coventry, Finch being made keeper, he was made chief justice of the common pleas, then the best office of the law, and that which he was wont to say, in his highest ambition, in his own private wishes, he had most desired; and it was indeed the sphere in which he moved most gracefully, and with most advantage, being a master of all that learning and knowledge which that place required, and an excellent judge, of great gravity, and above all suspicion of corruption. I. 209. 568.

---

#### SIR EDWARD HERBERT,* ATTORNEY GENERAL—— DIED MDCLVII.

HE was very unlike any other man; of a good natural wit, improved by conversation with learned men, but not at all by study and industry; and then his conversation was most with men, though much superior to him in parts, who rather admired, than informed him, of which his nature (being the proudest man living) made him not capable, because not desirous. His greatest faculty was, and in which he was a master, to make difficult matters more intricate and perplexed; and very easy things to seem more hard than they were. Charles II. (when in France) called him to his council, and made him lord keeper of the great

* His son Arthur was created earl of Torrington, and Edward was advanced to be lord chief justice of the king's bench.

seal, with which he seemed wonderfully delighted, and for some time lived well with every body; though, as to any thing of business, he appeared in his old excellent faculty of raising doubts. I. 210. III. 514. Life I. 175.

---

## LUCIUS CAREY, SECOND VISCOUNT FALKLAND; SECRETARY OF STATE—KILLED AT THE BATTLE OF NEWBURY MDCXLIII.

IF the celebrating the memory of eminent and extraordinary persons, and transmitting their great virtues for the imitation of posterity, be one of the principal ends and duties of history, it will not be thought impertinent, in this place, to remember a loss which no time will suffer to be forgotten, and no success or good fortune could repair. In this unhappy battle, was slain the lord viscount Falkland; a person of such prodigious parts of learning and knowledge, of that inimitable sweetness and delight in conversation, of so flowing and obliging a humanity and goodness to mankind, and of that primitive simplicity and inte-

L:d FAULKLAND

Pub.l 1794. by I.Herbert, 29 Russell St. Bloomsb---

grity of life, that if there were no other brand upon this odious and accursed civil war, than that single loss, it must be most infamous, and execrable to all posterity——

*Turpe mori, post te, solo non posse dolore.*

He was wonderfully beloved by all who knew him, as a man of excellent parts, of a wit so sharp, and a nature so sincere, that nothing could be more lovely.

His house (at Tew) being within little more than ten miles of Oxford, he contracted familiarity and friendship with the most polite and accurate men of that university; who found such an immenseness of wit, and such a solidity of judgment in him, so infinite a fancy, bound in by a most logical ratiocination; * such a vast knowledge, that he was not ignorant in any thing; yet such an excessive humility, as if he had known nothing; that they frequently resorted, and dwelt with him, as in a college situated in a purer air; so that his house was a university in a less volume, whither they came not so much for repose as study, and

* Although a perfect resemblance of Dr. Johnson is not to be found in any age, parts of his character are here admirably expressed. *Boswell's Johnson.* 4to. II. 587.

to examine and refine those grosser propositions, which laziness and consent made current in vulgar conversation.

He was superior to all those passions and affections which attend vulgar minds, and was guilty of no other ambition than of knowledge, and to be reputed a lover of all good men; and that made him too much a contemner of those arts, which must be indulged in the transactions of human affairs.

The great opinion he had of the uprightness and integrity of those persons who appeared most active, especially of Mr. Hampden, kept him longer from suspecting any design against the peace of the kingdom; and though he differed from them commonly in conclusions, he believed long their purposes were honest. When he grew better informed what was law, and discerned in them a desire to controul that law by a vote of one, or both houses, no man more opposed those attempts, and gave the adverse party more trouble by reason and argumentation; insomuch as he was, by degrees, looked upon as an advocate for the court, to which he contributed so little, that he declined those addresses, and even those invitations which he was obliged almost by civility to entertain. And he was so jealous of the least imagination that he should incline to preferment, that he affected even a moroseness to the court, and to the courtiers; and left nothing undone which might prevent, and divert the king's or queen's favour towards him, but the deserving it.

In the morning before the battle, as always upon action, he was very cheerful, and put himself into the first rank of the lord Byron's regiment, then advancing upon the enemy, who had lined the hedges on both sides with musqueteers; from whence he was shot with a musquet in the lower part of the belly, and in the instant falling from his horse, his body was not found till the next morning; till when, there was some hope he might have been a prisoner; though his nearest friends, who knew his temper, received small comfort from that imagination. Thus fell that incomparable young man, in the four-and-thirtieth year of his age, having so much dispatched the true business of life, that the oldest rarely attain to that immense knowledge, and the youngest enter not into the world with more innocency: whosoever leads such a life, needs be the less anxious upon how short warning it is taken from him.

His stature was low, and smaller than most men's; his motion not graceful; and his aspect so far from inviting, that it had somewhat in it of simplicity; and his voice the worst of the three, and so untuned, that instead of reconciling, it offended the ear; but that little person, and small stature, was quickly found to contain a great heart, a courage so keen, and a nature so fearless, that no composition of the strongest limbs ever disposed any man to greater enterprize; and that untuned tongue and voice, easily discovered itself to be supplied and governed by a mind and understanding so excellent, that the wit and weight of all he said, carried greater lustre with it than any ornament of delivery could ensure. I. 340. II. 350. Life I. 39.

## SIR JOHN COLEPEPPER, CHANCELLOR OF THE EX-CHEQUER*—DIED MDCLX.

HE had spent some years of his youth in foreign parts, and especially in armies, where he had seen good service, and very well observed it. He was proud and ambitious, and very much disposed to improve his fortune, which he knew well how to do by industry and thrift, without stooping to any corrupt ways, to which he was not inclined. He did not love the persons of many of those who were the violent managers; and less their designs: and therefore he no sooner knew that he was well spoken of at court, but he exposed himself to the invitation, and heartily embraced that interest. He had a wonderful insinuation and address into the acceptation and confidence of the king and queen, and was not suspected of flattery, when no man more complied with those infirmities they both had; and, by that compliance, prevailed often over them.

He was generally esteemed as a good speaker, being a man of an universal understanding, a quick

* Master of the rolls, and cr. baron Colepepper of Thoresway, co. Lincoln, 1644.

comprehension, a wonderful memory, who commonly spoke at the end of the debate; when he would recollect all that had been said of weight on all sides with great exactness, and express his own sense with much clearness, and such an application to the house, that no man more gathered a general concurrence to his opinion than he; which was the more notable, because his person, and manner of speaking were ungracious enough; so that he prevailed only by the strength of his reason, which was enforced with sufficient confidence. I. 340. Life I. 93.

---

GEORGE LORD DIGBY,* SUCCEEDED HIS FATHER AS EARL OF BRISTOL, MDCLIII.—DIED MDCLXXVI.

HE was a man of very extraordinary parts by nature and art, and had surely as good and excellent an education as any man of that age in any country: a graceful and beautiful person, of great

* Lord Digby advised the impeachment of lord Kimbolton, and the five members; to which *Hume* ascribes the disorders which followed.

eloquence and becomingness in his discourse (save that sometimes he seemed a little affected), and of so universal a knowledge, that he never wanted subject for a discourse: he was equal to a very good part in the greatest affairs, but the unfittest man alive to conduct them, having an ambition and vanity superior to all his other parts, and a confidence in himself, which sometimes intoxicated, transported, and exposed him. He had from his youth, by the disobligations his family had undergone from the duke of Buckingham, and the great men who succeeded him, and some sharp reprehension himself had met with, which obliged him to a country life, contracted a prejudice, and ill will to the court; and so had in the beginning of the parliament engaged himself with that party which discovered most aversion to it, with a passion and animosity equal to theirs, and therefore very acceptable to them. But when he was weary of their violent counsels, and withdrew himself from them, with some circumstances which enough provoked them, and made a reconciliation, and mutual confidence in each other for the future, manifestly impossible amongst them: he made private and secret offers of his service to the king.

to whom, in so general a defection of his servants, it could not but be very agreeable; and so his majesty being satisfied, both in the discoveries he made of what had passed, and in his professions for the future, removed him from the house of commons, where he had rendered himself marvellously ungracious, and called him by writ to the house of peers, where he did visibly advance the king's service. I. 343.

---

## JOHN WILLIAMS, ARCHBISHOP OF YORK[*]—DIED MDCXXXI.

HE was a man of a very imperious and fiery temper, had been bishop of Lincoln, and keeper of the great seal of England, in the time of king James. After his removal from that charge, he had lived splendidly in his diocess, and made himself very popular amongst those who had no reverence for the court; of which he would fre-

[*] The protestation signed by twelve of the bishops, and which occasioned their impeachment in 1642, was attributed to Williams.

quently, and in the presence of many, speak with too much freedom, and tell many stories of things and persons upon his own former experience; in which, being a man of great pride and vanity, he did not always confine himself to a precise veracity, and did often presume, in those unwary discourses, to mention the person of the king with too little reverence. He did affect to be thought an enemy to the archbishop of Canterbury; whose person he seemed exceedingly to contemn, and to be much displeased with those ceremonies and innovations, as they were then called, which were countenanced by the other; and had himself published, by his own authority, a book against the using those ceremonies; in which there was much good learning, and too little gravity for a bishop. His passion and his levity gave every day great advantages to those who did not love him, and he provoked too many, not to have those advantages made use of: so that, after several informations against him in the star-chamber, he was sentenced, and fined in a great sum of money to the king, and committed prisoner to the tower; without the pity or compassion of any, but those who, out of hatred to the government, were sorry that they were without so useful a champion; for he appeared to be a man of a very corrupt nature, whose passions could have transported him into the most unjustifiable actions. I. 345.

---

## WILLIAM SEYMOUR, MARQUIS OF HERTFORD; RESTORED TO THE DUKEDOM OF SOMERSET—DIED MDCLX.

HE was a man of great honour, interest, and estate, and of an universal esteem over the whole kingdom; and though he had received many and continued disobligations from the court, from the time of this king's coming to the crown, as well as during the reign of king James, in both which seasons, more than ordinary care had been taken to discountenance and lessen his interest; yet he had carried himself with notable steadiness, from the beginning of the parliament, in the support and defence of the king's power and dignity, notwithstanding all his allies, and those with whom he had the greatest familiarity and friendship, were of the opposite party; and never concurred with them against the earl of Strafford, whom he was known not to love, nor in any other extravagancy. He did accept the government of the prince of Wales, purely out of obedience to the king; and, no doubt, it was a great service; though for the performance of the office of a governor, he never thought himself fit, nor meddled with it. I. 425. II. 199.

---

ROBERT BERTIE, LORD WILLOUGHBY; CR. EARL OF LINDSEY, LORD GREAT CHAMBERLAIN—SLAIN AT EDGE-HILL MDCXLII.

HE was a man of very noble extraction, and inherited a great fortune from his ancestors; which though he did not manage with so great care, as if he desired much to improve, yet he left it in a very fair condition to his family, which more intended the increase of it. He was a man of great honour, and spent his youth and vigour of his age in military actions and commands abroad; and albeit he indulged to himself great liberties of life, yet he still preserved a very good reputation with all men, and a very great interest in his country, as appeared by the supplies he and his son brought to the king's army; the several companies of his own regiment of foot being commanded by the principal knights* and gentlemen of Lincolnshire, who engaged themselves in the service principally out of their personal affection to him. He was of a very generous nature, and punctual in what he undertook, and in exacting what was due to him; which made him bear that restriction so heavily which was put upon him by the commission granted to prince Rupert, and by the king's preferring the prince's opinion, in all matters relating to the war, before his. Nor did he conceal his resentment: the day before the battle, he said to some friends, with whom he had used freedom, " that he did not look upon himself as general; " and therefore he was resolved, when the day of " battle should come, that he would be in the head " of his regiment as a private colonel, where he

* Old Sir Gervase Scrope, who had received sixteen wounds, lay stripped among the dead above two days before his son could find him; an instance of great filial piety, and eminent loyalty! (the father died 1655; the son, Sir Adrian, K. B. died 1667). II. 56.

Vandyke pinx.                                W. I. Taylor scu.

*The Earl of Linds.*

Pub.d March 1. 1804 by I Herbert N.o 6 Pall M.

"would die." He was carried out of the field to the next village, and if he could then have procured surgeons, it was thought his wound would not have proved mortal. He had very many friends, and very few enemies; and died generally lamented. II. 52.

### GEORGE STUART, LORD AUBIGNEY (BROTHER TO THE DUKE OF RICHMOND)—SLAIN AT EDGEHILL MDCXLII.

HE was a gentleman of great hopes; of a gentle and winning disposition, and of very clear courage: he was killed in the first charge with the horse; where there being so little resistance, gave occasion to suspect that it was done by his own lieutenant, who was a Dutchman, and had not been so punctual in his duty, but that he received some reprehension from his captain, which he murmured at. His body was brought off, and buried at Christ-church in Oxford; his two younger brothers, the lord John and the lord Bernard Stuart, were in the same battle, and were afterwards both killed in the war, and his only son is now duke of Richmond. II. 53.

### ROBERT GREVILE, SECOND LORD BROOKE—SHOT AT LITCHFIELD MDCXLII.

HE lodged in a house within musquet-shot of the close; where, the very day he meant to assault it, sitting in his chamber, and the window open (just after he had prayed publicly, "that if the cause he were in were not right and just, he might be presently cut off"), he was, from the wall of the close, by a common soldier, shot with a musquet in the eye; of which he instantly died, without speaking a word.

They who were acquainted with him, believed him to be well-natured, and just; and rather seduced and corrupted in his understanding, than perverse and malicious. Whether his passions or conscience swayed him, he was undoubtedly one of those who could have been with most difficulty reconciled to the government of church or state: and therefore his death was looked upon as no ill omen to peace, and was exceedingly lamented by his party; which had scarce a more absolute confidence in any man than in him. II. 149.

L<sup>d</sup> NORTHAMPTON

## SPENCER COMPTON, SECOND EARL OF NORTHAMPTON; GENERAL OF THE KING'S ARMY—SLAIN AT HOPTON HEATH MDCXLII.

THE royal army, which had all the ensigns of victory but their general, thought themselves undone; whilst the other side, who had escaped in the night, and made a hard shift to carry his dead body with them, hardly believed they were losers:

*Et, velut æquali bellatum sorte fuisset,*
*Componit cum classe virum———*

The truth is, a greater victory had been an unequal recompence for such a loss. He was a person of great courage, honour, and fidelity, and not well known till his evening; having in the ease, and plenty, and luxury of that too happy time, indulged himself with that licence, which was then thought necessary to great fortunes: but from the beginning of these distractions, as if he had been awakened out of a lethargy, he never proceeded with a luke-warm temper. Before the standard was set up, he appeared in Warwickshire against the lord Brook, and as much upon his own reputation as the justice of the cause (which was not so well then understood) discountenanced, and drove him out of that county. Afterwards he took the ordnance from Banbury castle, and brought them to the king. As soon as an army was to be raised, he levied, with the first, upon his own charge, a troop of horse, and a regiment of foot, and (not like some other men, who warily distributed their family to both sides, one son to serve the king, whilst his father, or another son, engaged as far for the parliament) entirely dedicated all his children to the quarrel; having four sons officers under him, whereof three charged that day in the field: and from the time he submitted himself to the profession of a soldier, no man more punctual upon command, no man more diligent and vigilant in duty. All distresses he bore like a common man, and all wants and hardnesses, as if he had never known plenty or ease; most prodigal of his person to danger, and would often say, " that if he outlived these wars, he was certain 'never to have so noble a death." So that it is not to be wondered if, upon such a stroke, the body that felt it, thought it had lost more than a limb. II. 151.

## JAMES STUART, CR. DUKE OF RICHMOND——DIED MDCLV.

AS he was of the noblest extraction, being the nearest allied to the king's person of any man who was not descended from king James, so he was very worthy of all the grace and favour the king had shewed him. He was a man of very good parts, and an excellent understanding, yet, which is no common infirmity, so diffident of himself, that he was sometimes led by men who judged much worse. He was of a great and haughty spirit; and so punctual in point of honour, that he never swerved a tittle. He had so entire a resignation of himself to the king, that he abhorred all artifices to shelter himself from the prejudice of those, who, how powerful soever, failed in their duty to his majesty; and therefore he was pursued with all imaginable malice by them, as one that would have no quarter upon so infamous terms, as but looking on whilst his master was ill used. As he had received great bounties from the king, so he sacrificed all he had to his service, as soon as his occasions stood in need of it; and lent his majesty, at one time, twenty thousand pounds together; and, as soon as the war began, engaged his three brothers, all gallant gentlemen, in the service; in which they all lost their lives. Himself lived, with unspotted fidelity, some years after the murder of his master, and was suffered to put him into his grave; and died without the comfort of seeing the resurrection of the crown. II. 198. Life I. 185.

---

THOMAS WRIOTHESLEY, FOURTH EARL OF SOUTHAMPTON; LORD TREASURER AFTER THE RESTORATION*—DIED MDCLXVII.

HE was indeed a great man in all respects, and brought very much reputation to the king's cause. He had great dislike of the high courses which had been taken in the government, and a particular prejudice to the earl of Strafford, for some

* He and Lord C. Clarendon were firm friends, and had virtue and credit enough with Charles II. and at the board, to prevent, at least to defer, any very unreasonable resolution. The death of the former, opened a gap wide enough to let in all that ruin which overwhelmed the latter. Life III. 780.

exorbitant proceedings. But as soon as he saw the ways of reverence and duty towards the king declined, and the prosecution of the earl of Strafford to exceed the limits of justice, he opposed them vigorously in all their proceedings. He was a man of great sharpness of judgment, a very quick apprehension, and that readiness of expression upon any sudden debate, that no man delivered himself more advantageously, and weightily, and more efficaciously with the hearers; so that no man gave them more trouble in his opposition, or drew so many to a concurrence with him in opinion. He had no relation to, or dependence upon the court, or purpose to have any; but wholly pursued the public interest.

He was not only an exact observer of justice, but so clear-sighted a discerner of all the circumstances which might disguise it, that no false or fraudulent colour could impose upon him; and of so sincere and impartial a judgment, that no prejudice to the person of any man made him less awake to his cause; but believed that there is *aliquid et in hostem nefas*, and that a very ill man might be very unjustly dealt with. On the happy return of his majesty he seemed to recover great vigour of mind, and undertook the charge of high treasurer with much alacrity and industry, as long as he had any hope to get a revenue settled proportionable to the expence of the crown (towards which, his interest, and authority, and counsel, contributed very much), or to reduce the expence of the court within the limits of the revenue. His person was of a small stature; his courage, as all his other faculties, very great; having no sign of fear, or sense of danger, when he was in a place where he ought to be found. II. 200. Life. III. 781.

### ROBERT SIDNEY, SECOND EARL OF LEICESTER——DIED MDCLXXVII.

HE was a man of great parts, very conversant in books, and much addicted to the mathematics; and though he had been a soldier, and commanded a regiment, in the service of the states of the United Provinces, and was afterwards employed in several embassies, as in Denmark, and in France, was in truth rather a speculative, than a practical man; and expected a greater certitude in the consultation of business, than the business of this world is capable of: which temper proved very inconvenient to him through the course of his life. He was, after the death of the earl of Strafford, by the concurrent kindness and esteem both of king and queen, called from his embassy in France, to be lieutenant of Ireland; and in a very short time after, unhappily lost that kindness and esteem. He lay under many reproaches and jealousies which he deserved not; for he was a man of honour and fidelity to the king, and his greatest misfortunes proceeded from the staggering and irresolution of his nature. II. 201.

---

**JOHN LORD DIGBY OF SHERBORN, CR. EARL OF BRISTOL—DIED MDCLIII.**

HE was a man of a grave aspect, of a presence that drew respect, and of long experience in affairs of great importance. He had been, by the extraordinary favour of king James to his person (for he was a very handsome man) and his parts, which were naturally great, and had been improved by good education at home and abroad, sent ambassador into Spain, before he was thirty years of age. Though he was a man of great parts, and a wise man, yet he had been for the most part single, and by himself in business, which he managed with good sufficiency; and had lived little in consort, so that in council he was passionate and supercilious, and did not bear contradiction without much passion, and was too voluminous in discourse; so that he was not considered there with much respect; to the lessening whereof, no man contributed more than his son, the lord Digby; who shortly after came to sit there as secretary of state, and had not that reverence for his father's wisdom, which his great experience deserved, though he failed not in his piety towards him. II. 201

## WILLIAM CAVENDISH, CR. EARL, MARQUIS, AND DUKE OF NEWCASTLE——DIED MDCLXXVI.

HE was a very fine gentleman, active, and full of courage, and most accomplished in those qualities of horsemanship, dancing, and fencing, which accompany a good breeding; in which his delight was. Besides that, he was amorous in poetry and music, to which he indulged the greatest part of his time; and nothing could have tempted him out of those paths of pleasure, which he enjoyed in a full and ample fortune, but honour and ambition to serve the king when he saw him in distress, and abandoned by most of those who were in the highest degree obliged to him, and by him. He loved monarchy, as it was the foundation and support of his own greatness; and the church, as it was well constituted for the splendour and security of the crown; and religion, as it cherished and maintained that order and obedience that was necessary to both; without any other passion for the particular opinions which were grown up in it, and distinguished it into parties, than as he detested whatsoever was like to disturb the public peace.

He had a particular reverence for the person of the king, and a more extraordinary devotion for that of the prince, as he had had the honour to be trusted with his education, as his governor; for which office, as he excelled in some, so he wanted other qualifications. He liked the pomp and absolute authority of a general, and preserved the dignity of it to the full; and for the discharge of the outward state and circumstances of it, in acts of courtesy, affability, bounty, and generosity, he abounded; which in the infancy of a war became him, and made him for some time, very acceptable to men of all conditions: but the substantial part, and fatigue of a general, he did not in any degree understand. They who most exactly describe the unfortunate battle of Marston-moor, and the more unfortunate abandoning that whole country (when there might have been means found to have drawn a good army together) give so ill an account of any conduct or discretion in the managing of that affair, that, as I can take no pleasure in writing of it, so posterity would receive little pleasure, or benefit, in the most particular relation of it. II. 507.

## SIR CHARLES CAVENDISH——DIED MDCLIII.

HE was one of the most extraordinary persons of that age, in all the noble endowments of the mind. He had all the disadvantages imaginable in his person; which was not only of so small a size, that it drew the eyes of all men upon him; but with such deformity in his little person, and an aspect in his countenance, that was apter to raise contempt than applause; but in this unhandsome or homely habitation there was a mind and a soul lodged, that was very lovely and beautiful; cultivated and polished by all the knowledge and wisdom that arts and sciences could supply it with. He was a great philosopher, in the extent of it; and an excellent mathematician; whose correspondence was very dear to Gassendus and Descartes; the last of whom dedicated some of his works to him. He had a very notable courage; and the vigour of his mind so adorned his body, that " being with his brother, the marquis, in all the war," he usually went out in all parties; and was present, and charged the enemy in all battles, with as keen a courage as could dwell in the heart of man. But then the gentleness of his disposition, the humility and meekness of his nature, and the vivacity of his wit, were admirable. He was so modest, that he could hardly be prevailed with to enlarge himself on subjects which he understood better than other men, except he were pressed by his very familiar friends. Above all, his virtue and piety were such, that no temptation could work upon him to consent to any thing, that swerved in the least degree from the precise rules of honour, or the most severe rules of conscience. Life I. 250.

---

### SIR FRANCIS SEYMOUR, CR. LORD SEYMOUR OF TROWBRIDGE*——DIED MDCLXIV.

BEING brother to the marquis of Hertford, was a man of interest and reputation; he had been always very popular in the country; where he had lived out of the grace of the court; and his parts and judgment were best in those things which concerned the good husbandry, and the common ad-

* Chancellor of the dutchy of Lancaster, 1660.

ministration of justice to the people. Having a great friendship for the earl of Strafford, he was, by his interposition, called to the house of peers, where he carried himself very well in all things relating to the crown. II. 203.

---

THOMAS SAVILE, LORD SAVILE OF PONTEFRACT, CR. EARL OF SUSSEX—DIED MDCXLVI.

HE was likewise of the council, being first controller, and then treasurer of the household, in recompence of his discovery of all the treasons and conspiracies, after they had taken effect, and could not be punished. He was a man of an ambitious and restless nature; of parts and wit enough; but, in his disposition and inclination, so false, that he could never be believed or depended upon.

When the king came to York, where this lord's fortune and interest lay, his reputation was so low, that the gentlemen of interest, who wished well to the king's service, would not communicate with him; and, after the king's remove from thence, the earl of Newcastle found cause to have such a jealousy of him, that he thought it necessary to imprison him; and afterwards sent him to Oxford; where he so well purged himself, that he was again restored to his office. But in the end, he behaved himself so ill, that the king put him again out of his place, and committed him to prison, and never after admitted him to his presence; nor would any man of quality ever after keep any correspondence with him. II. 203.

---

### SIR EDWARD NICHOLAS, SECRETARY OF STATE——DIED MDCLXIX.

HE was a very honest and industrious man, and always versed in business, which few of the other were, or had been. After some time spent in the university of Oxford, and then in the Middle Temple, he lived some years in France; and was afterwards secretary to the lord Zouch, who was a privy counsellor, and warden of the Cinque Ports; and thereby he understood all that jurisdiction, which is very great, and exclusive to the admiral.

And when that lord, many years after, surrendered that office to the king, to the end that it might be conferred upon the duke of Buckingham, his secretary was likewise preferred with the office; and so, in a short time, became secretary of the admiralty, as well as of the Cinque Ports; and was entirely trusted and esteemed by that great favourite. After his death, he continued in the same place whilst the office was in commission, and was then made clerk of the council, from whence the king called him to be secretary of state,* after secretary Windebank fled the kingdom; upon his majesty's own observation of his virtue and fidelity, and without any other recommendation: and he was in truth, throughout his whole life, a person of very good reputation, and of singular integrity. II. 205.

* He was again appointed secretary of state at the restoration, and was a man of great gravity, and without any ambitious or private designs. Life II. 6.

## ALGERNON PERCY, FOURTH EARL OF NORTHUMBERLAND*——DIED MDCLXVIII.

HE was, in all his deportment, a very great man, and that which looked like formality, was a punctuality in preserving his dignity from the invasion and intrusion of bold men, which no man of that age so well preserved himself from. Though his notions were not large or deep, yet his temper and reservedness in discourse got him the reputation of an able and a wise man; which he made evident in the excellent government of his family, where no man was more absolutely obeyed; and no man had ever fewer idle words to answer for; and in debates of importance, he always expressed himself very pertinently. If he had thought the king as much above him, as he thought himself above other considerable men, he would have been a good subject; but the extreme undervaluing those, and not enough valuing the king, made him

* He was the chief of those of the king's council who stayed and acted with the parliament. The earls of Pembroke, Essex, Holland, Manchester, and lord Say, who took the same part, have been mentioned before.

liable to the impressions, which they who approached him by those addresses of reverence and esteem, that usually insinuate into such natures, made in him. So that after he was first prevailed upon, not to do that which in honour and gratitude he was obliged to (which is a very pestilent corruption), he was with the more facility led to concur in what, in duty and fidelity, he ought not to have done, and which at first he never intended to have done. And so he concurred in all the counsels which produced the rebellion, and stayed with them to support it. II. 206.

---

**WILLIAM CECIL, SECOND EARL OF SALISBURY——
DIED MDCLXVIII.**

HE had been born and bred in court, and had the advantage of a descent from a father and a grandfather who had been very wise men, and great ministers of state in the eyes of Christendom; whose wisdom and virtues died with them, and their children only inherited their titles. He had been admitted of the council to king James; from which time he continued so obsequious to the court, that he never failed in overacting all that he was required to do. No act of power was ever proposed, which he did not advance, and execute his part with the utmost rigour: no man so great a tyrant in his country, or was less swayed by any motives of justice or honour. He was a man of no words, except in hunting and hawking; in matters of state and council, he always concurred in what was proposed for the king; and cancelled and repaired all those transgressions by concurring in all that was proposed against him, as soon as any such propositions were made. Yet when the king went to York, he likewise attended upon his majesty; and at that distance, seemed to have recovered some courage, and concurred in all counsels which were taken to undeceive the people, and to make the proceedings of the parliament odious to all the world. But, on a sudden, he caused his horses to attend him out of the town, and having placed fresh ones at a distance, he fled back to London, with the expedition such men use when they are most afraid; and never after denied to do any thing that was required of him. And when the war was ended, and Cromwell had put down the house of peers, he got himself to be chosen a member of the house of commons; and sat with them, as of their own body; and was esteemed accordingly. II. 209.

---

**ROBERT RICH, THIRD EARL OF WARWICK——DIED MDCLVIII.**

HE was of the king's council too, but was not wondered at for leaving the king, whom he had never well served; nor did he look upon himself as obliged by that honour, which he knew was conferred upon him in the crowd of those whom his majesty had no esteem of, or ever proposed to trust; so his business was to join with those to whom he owed his promotion. He was a man of a pleasant and companionable wit and conversation; of an universal jollity, and such a licence in his words and in his actions, that a man of less virtue could not be found out; so that one might reasonably have believed, that a man so qualified, would not have been able to have contributed much to the overthrow of a nation and kingdom.

But with all these faults, he had great authority and credit with that people who, in the beginning of the troubles, did all the mischief; and by opening his doors, and making his house the rendezvous of all the silenced ministers, in the time when there was authority to silence them, and spending a good part of his estate, of which he was very prodigal, upon them, and by being present with them at their devotions, and making himself merry with them, and at them, which they dispensed with, he became the head of that party; and got the style of a godly man. When the king revoked the earl of Northumberland's commission of admiral, he presently accepted the office from the parliament; and never quitted their service; and when Cromwell disbanded that parliament, he betook himself to the protection of the protector; married his heir to his daughter; and lived in so entire a confidence and friendship with him, that when the protector died, he exceedingly lamented him. He left his estate, which before was subject to a vast debt, more improved and repaired than any man who trafficked in that desperate commodity, rebellion. II. 210.

## SIR HENRY VANE THE ELDER, SECRETARY OF STATE——DIED MDCLIII.

HE was the last of the counsellors who stayed with the parliament, and had so much excuse for it, that, being thrown out of court, he had no where else to go; and promised himself to be made much of by them, for whose sakes only he had brought that infamy upon himself. He was of very ordinary parts by nature, and had not cultivated them at all by art; for he was illiterate. But being of a stirring and boisterous disposition, very industrious, and very bold, he still wrought himself into some employment. He had been controller of the household; which place he became well, and was fit for, and if he had never taken other preferment, he might probably have continued a good subject: for he had not inclination to change, and in his judgment he had liked the government both in church and state; and only desired to raise his fortune, which was not great, and which he found many ways to improve. As the fatal preferring him to the post of secretary of state was of unspeakable prejudice to the king, so his receiving it was to his own destruction. His malice to the earl of Strafford (who had unwisely provoked him, wantonly and out of contempt *) transported him to all imaginary thoughts of revenge; which is a guest that naturally disquiets and tortures those who entertain it, with all the perplexities they contrive for others; and that disposed him to sacrifice his honour and faith, and his master's interest, that he might ruin the earl, and was buried himself in the same ruin; for which being justly chastised by the king, and turned out of his service, he was left to his own despair: and though he concurred in all the malicious designs against the king, and against the church, he grew into the hatred and contempt of those who had made most use of him, and died in universal reproach, and was not contemned more by any of his enemies, than by his own son, who had been his principal conductor to destruction. II. 213.

* See page 52.

### SIR BEVIL GRENVILLE——KILLED AT THE BATTLE OF LANSDOWN MDCXLIII.

THAT which would have clouded any victory, and made the loss of others less spoken of, was the death of Sir Bevil Grenville. He was indeed an excellent person, whose activity, interest, and reputation, were the foundation of what had been done in Cornwall; and his temper and affections, so public, that no accident which happened could make any impressions on him; and his example kept others from taking any thing ill, or at least seeming to do so. In a word, a brighter courage, and a gentler disposition, were never married together, to make the most cheerful and innocent conversation. II. 284.

---

### SIR NICHOLAS SLANNING—KILLED AT THE SIEGE OF BRISTOL MDCXLIII.

HE was governor of Pendennis castle, upon the credit and security whereof, the king's party in that country first depended, and by the command it had of the harbour of Falmouth, was, or might be, supplied with all that was necessary. He was indeed a young man of admirable parts, a sharp and discerning wit, a staid and solid judgment, a gentle and most obliging behaviour, and a courage so clear and keen, as, even without the other ornaments, would have rendered him very considerable. II. 298.

---

**WILLIAM VILLIERS, LORD VISCOUNT GRANDISON —KILLED AT THE SIEGE OF BRISTOL MDCXLIII.**

HE was a young man of so virtuous a habit of mind, that no temptation or provocation could corrupt him; so great a lover of justice and integrity, that no example, necessity, or even the barbarity of this war, could make him swerve from the most precise rules of it; and of that rare piety and devotion, that the court or camp could not shew a more faultless person, or to whose example young men might more reasonably conform themselves. His personal valour, and courage of all

kinds (for he had sometimes indulged so much to the corrupt opinion of honour, as to venture himself in duels) was very eminent, insomuch as he was accused of being too prodigal of his person: his affection, and zeal, and obedience to the king, were such as became a branch of that family; and he was wont to say, "that if he had not under-
"standing enough to know the uprightness of
"the cause, nor loyalty enough to inform him
"of the duty of a subject, yet the very obli-
"gations of gratitude to the king, on the be-
"half of his house, were such, as his life was
"but a due sacrifice:" and therefore, he no sooner saw the war unavoidable, than he engaged all his brethren,\* as well as himself, in the service; and there were then three more of them in command in the army when he was so unfortunately cut off. II. 299.

\* Amongst whom was Mr. Edward Villiers (ancestor of the present earls of Jersey and Clarendon) whose diligence and dexterity his majesty found fit for any trust. I. 666.

ROBERT LORD DORMER, CR. EARL OF CARNARVON——SLAIN AT THE BATTLE OF NEWBURY MDCXLIII.

HE was a person with whose great parts and virtue the world was not enough acquainted. Before the war, though his education was adorned by travel, and an exact observation of the manners of more nations than our common travellers use to visit (for he had, after the view of Spain, France, and most parts of Italy, spent some time in Turkey, and those eastern countries) he seemed to be wholly delighted with those looser exercises of pleasure—hunting, hawking, and the like, in which the nobility of that time too much delighted to excel. After the troubles begun, having the command of the first or second regiment of horse that was raised for the king's service, he wholly gave himself up to the office and duty of a soldier; no man more diligently obeying, or more dexterously commanding; for he was not only of a very keen courage in the exposing his person, but an excellent discerner and pursuer of advantage upon his enemy. He had a mind

Harding sculp. Vandyke pinx.

*Lord Carnarvon?*

Pub.d by I.Herbert 1794.

and understanding very present in the article of danger, which is a rare benefit in that profession. He was a great lover of justice, and practised it then most deliberately, when he had power to do wrong: and so strict in the observation of his word and promise, as a commander, that he could not be persuaded to stay in the west, when he found it not in his power to perform the agreement he had made with Dorchester and Weymouth. If he had lived, he would have proved a great ornament to that profession, and an excellent soldier; and by his death the king found a sensible weakness in his army. II. 349.

---

LORD JOHN STUART, GENERAL OF THE HORSE; AND SIR JOHN SMITH, BROTHER TO LORD CARRINGTON; COMMISSARY GENERAL OF THE HORSE—SLAIN AT THE BATTLE OF CHERITON DOWN, MDCXLIV.

THE former was a young man of extraordinary hope, little more than one-and-twenty years of age; who being of a more choleric and rough nature than the other branches of that illustrious and princely family, was not delighted with the softnesses of the court, but had dedicated himself to the profession of arms, when he did not think the scene should have been in his own country. His courage was so signal that day, that too much could not be expected from it, if he had outlived it; and he was so generally beloved, that he could not but be very generally lamented. The other, Sir John Smith, had been trained up from his youth in the war of Flanders; being of an ancient roman-catholic family; and had long the reputation of one of the best officers of horse. As soon as the first troubles appeared in Scotland, he betook himself to the service of his own prince; and from the beginning of the war to his own end, performed many signal actions of courage. The death of these two eminent officers, made the names of many who perished that day the less inquired into and mentioned. II. 475.

**PATRICK RUTHEN, GENERAL OF THE KING'S ARMY; CR. EARL OF BRENTFORD—DIED MDCLI.**

THOUGH he had been, without doubt, a very good officer, and had great experience, and was still a man of unquestionable courage and integrity; yet he was now (1644) much decayed in his parts, and, with the long continued custom of immoderate drinking, dozed in his understanding, which had been never quick and vigorous; he having been always illiterate to the greatest degree that can be imagined. He was now become very deaf, yet often pretended not to have heard what he did not then contradict, and thought fit afterwards to disclaim. He was a man of few words, and of great compliance, and usually delivered that as his opinion, which he foresaw would be grateful to the king. II. 481.

PRINCE RUPERT——DIED MDCLXXXII.

HE was rough and passionate, and loved not debate; liked what was proposed, as he liked the persons who proposed it; and was so great an enemy to Digby and Colepepper, who were only present in the debates of the war with the officers, that he crossed all they proposed. The truth is, all the army had been disposed, from the first raising it, to a neglect and contempt of the council; and the king himself had not been solicitous enough to preserve the respect due to it, in which he lessened his own dignity. II. 554.

---

HENRY VISCOUNT WILMOT, * GENERAL OF THE HORSE, COMPARED WITH HIS RIVAL AND SUCCESSOR, GEORGE LORD GORING. †

WILMOT loved debauchery, but shut it out from his business; never neglected that, and rarely

* He was created earl of Rochester, and died 1659.
† Eldest son of the earl of Norwich; he assumed the habit of a dominican friar in Spain, where he died.

miscarried in it. Goring had a much better understanding, and a sharper wit (except in the very exercise of debauchery, and then the other was inspired), a much keener courage, and presentness of mind in danger: Wilmot discerned it farther off, and because he could not behave himself so well in it, commonly prevented, or warily declined it; and never drank when he was within distance of an enemy: Goring was not able to resist the temptation when he was in the middle of them, nor would decline it to obtain a victory.

Neither of them valued their promises, professions, or friendships, according to any rules of honour or integrity; but Wilmot violated them the less willingly, and never but for some great benefit or convenience to himself: Goring without scruple, out of humour, or for wit's sake; and loved no man so well but that he would cozen him, and then expose him to public mirth for having been cozened: therefore he had always fewer friends than the other, but more company; for no man had a wit that pleased the company better. The ambition of both was unlimited, and so equally incapable of being contented; and both unrestrained by any respect to good nature or justice, from pursuing the satisfaction thereof: yet Wilmot had more scruples from religion to startle him, and would not have attained his end by any gross or foul act of wickedness; Goring could have passed through those pleasantly; and would, without hesitation, have broken any trust, or done any act of treachery, to have satisfied an ordinary passion or appetite; and in truth, wanted nothing but industry (for he had wit, and courage, and understanding, and ambition, uncontrouled by any fear of God or man) to have been as eminent and successful in the highest attempt of wickedness, as any man in the age he lived in, or before. Of all his qualifications, dissimulation was his master-piece; in which he so much excelled, that men were not ordinarily ashamed or out of countenance, with being deceived but twice by him. II. 481. 554.

L.d HOPTON

RALPH HOPTON, CR. LORD HOPTON OF STRATTON
——DIED MDCLII.

HE was a man superior to any temptation, and abhorred enough the license and the levities with which he saw too many corrupted. He had a good understanding, a clear courage, an industry not to be tired, and a generosity that was not to be exhausted, a virtue that none of the rest had; but in the debates concerning the war, was longer in resolving, and more apt to change his mind after he had resolved, than is agreeable to the office of a commander in chief; which rendered him rather fit for the second, than for the supreme command, in an army. II. 482.

———

SIR JACOB ASTLEY, CR. LORD ASTLEY——DIED MDCLI.

HE was an honest, brave, plain man, and as fit for the office he exercised, of major-general of the foot, as christendom yielded, and was so generally esteemed; very discerning and prompt in giving orders, as the occasions required, and most cheerful and present in any action. In council he used few, but very pertinent words; and was not at all pleased with the long speeches usually made there; and which rather confounded, than informed his understanding: so that he rather collected the ends of the debates, and what he was himself to do, than enlarged them by his own discourses; though he forbore not to deliver his own mind. II. 482.

---

### GEORGE BRYDGES, SIXTH LORD CHANDOS OF SUDLEY CASTLE——DIED MDCLIV.

HE was a young man of spirit and courage; and had, for two years, served the king very bravely at the head of a regiment of horse, which himself had raised at his own charge; but had lately, out of pure weariness of the fatigue, and having spent most of his money, and without any diminution of his affection, left the king, under pretence of travel; but making London his way, he gave himself up to the pleasures of that place; which he enjoyed without considering the issue of the war, or shewing any inclination to the parliament; nor did he, in any degree, contribute to the delivery of his house; which was at first imagined, because it was so ill, or not at all defended.* II. 491.

---

### SIR WILLIAM MORTON——DIED MDCLXXII.

HE was a gentleman of the long robe; who, in the beginning of the war, cast off his gown, as many other gallant men of that profession did, and served as lieutenant colonel in the regiment of horse under the lord Chandos; and had given so frequent testimony of signal courage in several actions, in which he had received many wounds, both by the pistol and the sword, that his mettle was never suspected; and his fidelity as little questioned: and after many years of imprisonment, sustained with great firmness and constancy, he lived

* Sudley castle was surrendered to Waller by treachery; and the governor, Sir William Morton, was sent to the Tower.

to receive the reward of his merit, after the return of the king; who made him first a serjeant at law; and afterwards a judge of the king's bench; \* where he sat many years, and discharged the office with much gravity and learning; and was very terrible to those who chose to live by robbing on the highway. II. 491.

---

SIR WILLIAM PENNYMAN, †—DIED S. P. MDCXLIII.

HE had been governor of Oxford, to the great satisfaction of all men, being a very brave and generous person, and who performed all manner of civilities to all sorts of people, as having had a good education, and well understanding the manners of the court. II. 526.

\* The portraits of judges *Kelyng, Twisden, Windham,* and *Morton,* of the king's bench; *Bridgeman, Tyrrell, Brown,* and *Archer,* of the common pleas; *Hale, Athyns, Turner,* and *Rainsford,* of the exchequer, (who offered to settle, without lawsuits, the disputes occasioned by the fire of London, in 1666) are in Guildhall.

† Of Marske, co. York; cr. a baronet, 1628. He was colonel of a regiment of foot; and in the civil wars maintained two troops of horse, and one company of foot, at his

## SIR HENRY GAGE, GOVERNOR OF OXFORD—KILLED NEAR ABINGDON, MDCXLIV.

HE was in truth a very extraordinary man, of a large and very graceful person; of an honourable extraction, his grandfather having been knight of the garter; besides his great experience and abilities as a soldier, which were very eminent, he had very great parts of breeding, being a very good scholar in the polite parts of learning, a great master in the Spanish and Italian tongues, besides the French and the Dutch, which he spoke in great perfection; having scarce been in England in twenty years before. He was likewise very conversant in courts, and deserved to be looked upon as a wise and accomplished person. Of this gentleman, the lords of the council had a singular esteem, and consulted frequently with him, whilst they looked to be besieged; and thought Oxford to be the more secure for his being in it. II. 527.

own expence. His cousin-german, James Pennyman, of Ormsby, was also a col. of foot in the king's army, and was created a baronet, 1663. *Wotton's Baronetage.*

### SIR HENRY KILLIGREW———DIED MDCXLVI.

HE was a member of the house of commons; and though he had no other relation to the court than the having many friends there, as wherever he was known he was exceedingly beloved, he was most zealous and passionate in opposing all the extravagant proceedings of the parliament.

He would never take any command in the army; but they who had, consulted with no man more. He was in all actions, and in those places where was most danger, having great courage and a pleasantness of humour in danger that was very exemplary; and they who did not do their duty, took care not to be within his view; for he was a very sharp speaker, and cared not for angering those who deserved to be reprehended. The Arundels, Trelawnies, Slannings, Trevanions, and all the signal men of that county, infinitely loved his spirit and sincerity; and his credit and interest had a great influence upon all but those who did not love the king; and to those he was very terrible, and exceedingly hated by them; and not loved by men of moderate tempers; for he thought all such prepared to rebel, when a little success should encourage them; and was many times too much offended with men who wished well, and whose constitutions and complexions would not permit them to express the same frankness, which his nature and keenness of spirit could not suppress. His loss was much lamented by all good men. III. 41.

---

**WILLIAM, DUKE OF HAMILTON—KILLED AT WORCESTER FIGHT, MDCLI.**

HE fell into the enemy's hands, and the next day died of his wounds; and thereby prevented the being made a spectacle, as his brother had been;* which the pride and animosity of his enemies would no doubt have caused to be, having the same pretence for it, by his being a peer of England, as the other was. He was, in all respects, to be much preferred before the other; a much wiser, though, it may be, a less cunning man: for he did not affect dissimulation, which

* Page 57.

was the other's master-piece. He had unquestionable courage: he was in truth a very accomplished person, of an excellent judgment, and clear and ready expressions: and though he had been driven into some unwarrantable actions, he made it very evident he had not been led by any inclinations of his own, and passionately and heartily run to all opportunities of redeeming it: and in the very article of his death, he expressed a marvellous cheerfulness, " that he had the ho-
" nour to lose his life in the king's service, and
" thereby to wipe out the memory of his former
" transgressions;" which he always professed were odious to himself. III. 124. 409.

---

JOHN MAITLAND, EARL OF LAUDERDALE; CR. DUKE——DIED MDCLXXXII.

HE was a man of great parts and industry, though he loved pleasure; but was insolent, imperious, flattering, and dissembling, fit for intrigues and contrivances, by the want of ingenuity,

Sr. Cha. LUCAS.

Pub.1 Nov.r 1794 by I.Herbert 29 Russell St Bloom

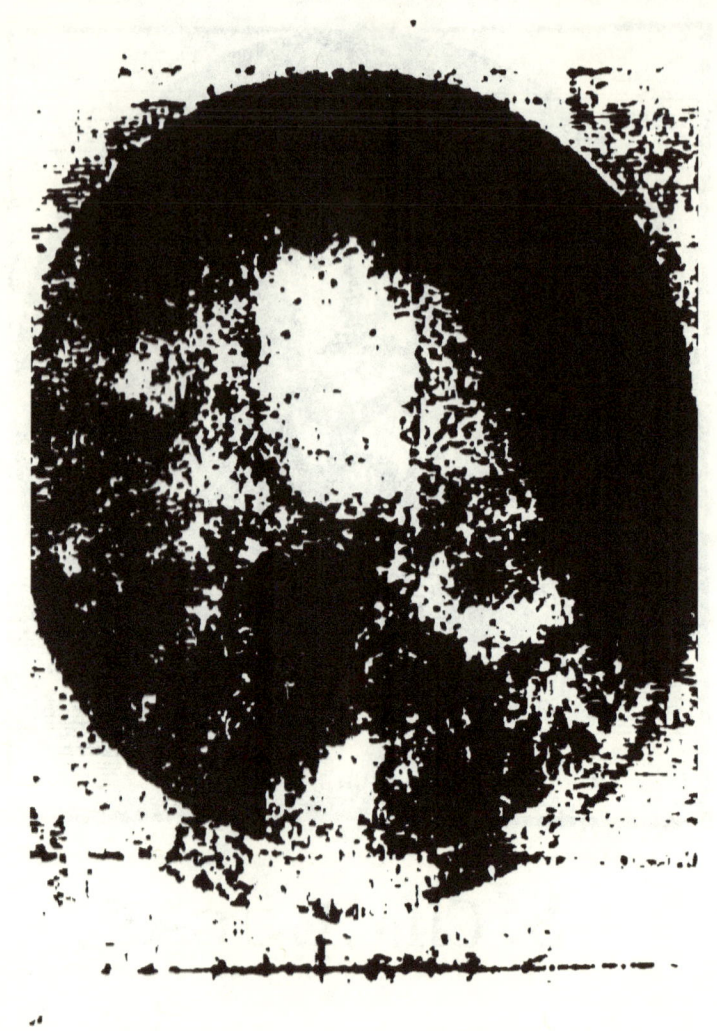

S.<sup>r</sup> Geo. LISLE.

and by the experience and practice he had in the committee of both kingdoms in their darkest designs. He had courage enough not to fail where it was absolutely necessary, and no impediment of honour to restrain him from doing any thing that might gratify any of his passions. III. 124.

---

SIR CHARLES LUCAS, AND SIR GEORGE LISLE—EXECUTED AT COLCHESTER, MDCXLVIII.

THEY were men of great name and esteem in the war; the one being held as good a commander of horse, and the other of foot, as the nation had; but of very different tempers and humours. Lucas was the younger brother of lord Lucas, and his heir both to the honour and estate, and had a present fortune of his own. He had been bred in the Low Countries under the prince of Orange, and always amongst the horse. He had little conversation in that court, where great civility was practised, and learned. He was very brave in his person, and in a day of battle a gallant man to look upon, and follow; but at all other times and places, of a nature scarce to be lived with, of no good understanding, of a rough and proud humour, and very morose conversation; yet they all desired to accompany him in his death. Lisle was a gentleman who had had the same education with the other, and at the same time an officer of foot; had all the courage of the other, and led his men to a battle with such an alacrity, that no man was ever better followed; his soldiers never forsaking him; and the party which he commanded, never left any thing undone which he led them upon. But then, to his fierceness of courage, he had the softest and most gentle nature imaginable; was kind to all, and beloved of all, and without a capacity to have an enemy. The manner of taking the lives of these worthy men was new, and without example, and concluded by most men to be very barbarous; and was generally imputed to Ireton, who swayed Fairfax, and was, upon all occasions, of an unmerciful and bloody nature. III. 178.

L.b CAPEL.

Pub 1 Oct 1794 by I Herbert 29 Russell str.

## ARTHUR CAPEL, CR. LORD CAPEL——BEHEADED MDCXLVIII.

HE was a man in whom the malice of his enemies could discover very few faults, and whom his friends could not wish better accomplished; whom Cromwell's own character well described, and who indeed would never have been contented to have lived under that government. His memory, all men loved and reverenced, though few followed his example. He had always lived in a state of great plenty and general estimation, having a very noble fortune of his own by descent, and a fair addition to it by his marriage with an excellent wife,* a lady of very worthy extraction, of great virtue and beauty, by whom he had a numerous issue of both sexes, in which he took great joy and comfort: so that no man was more happy in all his domestic affairs; and he was so much the more happy, in that he thought himself most blessed in them.

* Elizabeth, daughter and heir of Sir Charles Morison, knight and baronet. Her eldest son, Arthur, was created viscount Malden and earl of Essex.

And yet the king's honour was no sooner violated, and his just power invaded, than he threw all those blessings behind him; and having no other obligations to the crown, than those which his own honour and conscience suggested to him, he frankly engaged his person and his fortune from the beginning of the troubles, as many others did, in all actions and enterprizes of the greatest hazard and danger; and continued to the end, without ever making one false step, as few others did, though he had once, by the iniquity of a faction that then prevailed, an indignity put upon him that might have excused him for some remission of his former warmth. But it made no other impression upon him than to be quiet and contented, whilst they would let him alone, and, with the same cheerfulness, to obey the first summons when he was called out; which was quickly after. In a word, he was a man, that whoever shall, after him, deserve best of the English nation, he can never think himself undervalued, when he shall hear, that his courage, virtue, and fidelity, are laid in the balance with, and compared to that of the lord Capel. III. 273.

## Marquis of Montrose

Pub Mar 1 1796 by I Herbert

## JAMES GRAHAM, MARQUIS OF MONTROSE——EXECUTED AT EDINBURGH MDCL.

HE had given as great testimony of loyalty and courage as a subject could do, and performed as wonderful actions in several battles, upon as great inequality of numbers, and as great disadvantages in respect of arms, and other preparations for war, as have been performed in any age. He was a gentleman of a very ancient extraction, many of whose ancestors had exercised the highest charges under the king in Scotland, and had been allied to the crown itself. He was of very good parts, which were improved by a good education. He had always a great emulation, or rather a great contempt of the marquis of Argyle (as he was too apt to contemn those he did not love), who wanted nothing but honesty and courage to be a very extraordinary man, having all other good talents in a very great degree. Montrose was in his nature fearless of danger, and never declined any enterprize for the difficulty of going through with it, but exceedingly affected those which seemed desperate to other men, and did believe somewhat to be in himself above other men, which made him live more easily towards those who were, or were willing to be, inferior to him (towards whom he exercised wonderful civility and generosity), than with his superiors or equals. He was naturally jealous, and suspected those who did not concur with him in the way, not to mean so well as he. He was not without vanity, but his virtues were much superior, and he well deserved to have his memory preserved, and celebrated amongst the most illustrious persons of the age in which he lived. III. 357.

---

WILLIAM WIDDRINGTON, CR. LORD WIDDRINGTON\*—SLAIN AT WIGAN MDCLI.

HE was of the best and most ancient extraction of the county of Northumberland, and of a very fair fortune, and one of the four which Charles I. made choice of to be about the person of his son the prince, as gentleman of his privy-chamber, when he first settled his family. His affection to

\* Of Blankney, co. Lincoln.—Title forfeited, 1715.

the king was always remarkable; and serving in the house of commons, as knight of the shire, for the county of Northumberland, he quickly got the reputation of being amongst the most malignant. As soon as the war broke out, he was of the first who raised both horse and foot at his own charge, and served eminently with them under the marquis of Newcastle; with whom he had a very particular and entire friendship. He was very nearly allied to the marquis; and by his testimony that he had performed many signal services, he was, about the middle of the war, made a peer of the kingdom. He was a man of great courage, but of some passion, by which he incurred the ill-will of many, who imputed it to an insolence of nature, which no man was farther from; no man of a nature more civil, and candid towards all, in business, or conversation. But having sat long in the house of commons, and observed the disingenuity of the proceedings there, and the gross cheats by which they deceived and cozened the people, he had contracted so hearty an indignation against them, and all who were cozened by them, and against all who had not his zeal to oppose and destroy them, that he often said things to slow and phlegmatic men, which offended them, and, it may be, injured them; which his good-nature often obliged him to acknowledge, and ask pardon of those who would not question him for it. III. 404.

---

### SIR THOMAS TILDESLEY——SLAIN AT WIGAN MDCLI.

HE was a gentleman of a good family, and a good fortune; who had raised men at his own charge at the beginning of the war, and had served in the command of them till the very end of it, with great courage; and refusing to make any composition after the murder of the king, he found means to transport himself into Ireland to the marquis of Ormond; with whom he staid, till he was, with the rest of the English officers, dismissed, to satisfy the barbarous jealousy of the Irish; and then got over into Scotland, a little before the king marched from thence, and was desired by the earl of Derby to remain with him. III. 405.

Vandyke P.t    adam sculp.

## L.d DERBY.

*The Original at Cornbury L.d Clarendons.*

*Pub. May 1. 1794 by I. Herbert, Pall Mall.*

## JAMES STANLEY, SEVENTH EARL OF DERBY—— BEHEADED MDCLI.

He was a man of unquestionable loyalty to the late king, and gave clear testimony of it before he received any obligations from the court, and when he thought himself disobliged by it. Charles II. in his first year, sent him the garter; and the sense of that honour made him so readily comply with the king's command in attending him, when he had no confidence in the undertaking, nor any inclination to the Scots; who, he thought, had too much guilt upon them, in having depressed the crown, to be made instruments of repairing and restoring it. He was a man of great honour and clear courage; and all his defects and misfortunes, proceeded from his having lived so little time among his equals, that he knew not how to treat his inferiors; which was the source of all the ill that befel him, having thereby drawn such prejudice against him from persons of inferior quality, who yet thought themselves too good to be contemned, that they pursued him to death. The king's army was no sooner defeated at Worcester, but the parliament renewed their old method of murdering in cold blood, and sent a commission to erect a high court of justice to persons of ordinary quality, many not being gentlemen, and all notoriously his enemies, to try the earl of Derby for his treason and rebellion, which they easily found him guilty of; and put him to death in a town of his own\* (against which he had expressed a severe displeasure for their obstinate rebellion against the king), with all the circumstances of rudeness and barbarity they could invent. III. 411.

---

### HENRY IRETON——DIED MDCLI.

HE was of a melancholic, reserved, dark nature, who communicated his thoughts to very few; so that, for the most part, he resolved alone, but was never diverted from any resolution he had taken; and he was thought often by his obstinacy to pre-

\* Bolton in Lancashire.

vail over Cromwell himself, and to extort his concurrence contrary to his own inclinations: But that proceeded only from his dissembling less; for he was never reserved in the owning and communicating his worst and most barbarous purposes; which the other always concealed and disavowed. Hitherto their concurrence had been very natural, since they had the same ends and designs. It was generally conceived by those who had the opportunity to know them both very well, that Ireton was a man so radically averse to monarchy, and so fixed to a republican government, that, if he had lived, he would either, by his counsel and credit, have prevented those excesses in Cromwell, or, publicly opposed and declared against them, and carried the greatest part of the army with him; and that Cromwell, who best knew his nature, and his temper, had therefore carried him into Ireland, and left him there, that he might be without his counsels or importunities, when he should find it necessary to put off his mask, and to act that part which he foresaw it would be requisite to do. Others thought, his parts lay more towards civil affairs; and were fitter for the modelling that government, which his heart was set upon (being a scholar, conversant in the law, and in all those authors who had expressed the greatest animosity and malice against the regal government), than for the conduct of an army to support it; his personal courage being never reckoned among his other abilities. III. 467.

## JOHN WILDMAN——DIED MDC**

HE had been bred in the university of Cambridge; and being young, and of a pregnant wit, in the beginning of the rebellion meant to make his fortune in the war; and chose to depend upon Cromwell's countenance and advice, and was much esteemed and valued by him, and made an officer; and was so active in contriving and fomenting jealousies and discontents, and so dextrous in composing, or improving any disgusts, and so inspired with the spirit of praying and preaching, when those gifts came into request, and became thriving arts, that about the time when the king was taken from Holmby, and it was necessary that the army should enter into contests with the parliament, John Wildman grew to be one of the principal agitators, and was most relied upon by Cromwell to infuse those things into the minds of the soldiers, and to conduct them in the managery of their discontents, as might most advance those designs he then had; and quickly got the reputation of a man of parts; and, having a smooth pen, drew many of the papers which first kindled the fire between the parliament and the army, that was not afterwards extinguished but in the ruin of both. III. 499.

---

JOHN LILBURN——DIED MDCLVII.

BEFORE the troubles, he was a poor bookbinder; when the war begun, he put himself into the army, and was taken prisoner by the King's forces at Brentford, in 1642: and (being arraigned for treason) he behaved himself with so great impudence, in extolling the power of the parliament, that it was manifest he had an ambition to have been made a martyr for that cause. But as he was liberally supplied from his friends at London, (and the parliament in express terms declared, "that they would inflict punishment upon the prisoners they had of the king's party, in the same manner as Lilburn and the rest should suffer at Oxford") so he did find means to corrupt the marshal who had the custody of him; and made his escape into the parliament's quarters; where he was received with public joy, as a champion that had defied the king in his own court.

From this time he was entertained by Cromwell with great familiarity, and, in his contests with the parliament, was of much use to him, and privacy with him. But he begun then to find him of so restless and unruly a spirit, and to make those advances in religion against the presbyterians before he thought it seasonable, that he dispensed with his presence in the army, where he was an officer of name, and made him reside in London, where he wished that temper should be improved. III. 501.

### ROBERT BLAKE, ADMIRAL——DIED MDCLVII.*

HE was a man of a private extraction; yet had enough left him by his father to give him a good education; which his own inclination disposed him to receive in the university of Oxford; where he took the degree of a master of arts; and was enough versed in books for a man who intended not to be of any profession, having sufficient of his own to maintain him in the plenty he affected.

When the troubles begun, he quickly declared himself against the king; and having some command in Bristol, when it was first taken by prince Rupert and the marquis of Hertford, being trusted with the command of a little fort upon the line, he refused to give it up, after the governor had signed the articles of surrender, and kept it some hours after the prince was in the town, and killed some of the soldiers; for which the prince resolved to hang him, if some friends had not interposed for him, upon his want of experience in war; and

---

* Cromwell caused him to be buried in Henry VII. chapel, at the charge of the public.

prevailed with him to quit the place by very great importunity, and with much difficulty. After this, (having done eminent service to the parliament, especially at Taunton, at land), he betook himself wholly to the sea; and quickly made himself signal there. He was the first man that declined the old track, and made it manifest that the science might be attained in less time than was imagined; and despised those rules which had been long in practice, to keep his ship and his men out of danger; which had been held in former times a point of great ability and circumspection; as if the principal art requisite in the captain of a ship had been to be sure to come home safe again. He was the first man who brought the ships to contemn castles on shore, which had been thought ever very formidable, and were discovered by him to make a noise only, and to fright those who could rarely be hurt by them. He was the first that infused that proportion of courage into the seamen, by making them see by experience, what mighty things they could do, if they were resolved; and taught them to fight in fire as well as upon water: and though he hath been very well imitated and followed, he was the first that gave the

tation, had a greater influence upon the people, than they who talked more and louder; and was known to be irreconcilable to the new government; and therefore was cut off, notwithstanding very great intercession to preserve him.  III. 623.

---

JOHN HEWIT, D. D.——BEHEADED MDCLVIII.

HE was born a gentleman, and bred a scholar, and was a divine before the beginning of the troubles. He lived in Oxford, and in the army, till the end of the war, and continued afterwards to preach with great applause in a little church in London; where, by the affection of the parish, he was admitted, since he was enough known to lie notoriously under the brand of malignity. He was made choice of, to marry the Lord Falconbridge to Cromwell's daughter, according to the order of the church; which engaged both that lord and lady to use their utmost credit with the protector to preserve his life; but he was inexorable, and desirous that the churchmen, upon whom he looked as his mortal enemies, should see what they were to trust to, if they stood in need of his mercy. 'III. 624.

---

### OLIVER CROMWELL, LORD PROTECTOR——DIED MDCLVIII.

HE was one of those men, *quos vituperare ne inimici quidem possunt, nisi ut simul laudent;* whom his very enemies could not condemn without commending him at the same time: for he could never have done half that mischief without great parts of courage, industry, and judgment. He must have had a wonderful understanding in the natures and humours of men, and as great a dexterity in applying them; who, from a private and obscure birth (though of a good family) without interest or estate, alliance or friendship, could raise himself to such a height, and compound and knead such opposite and contradictory tempers, humours, and interests into a consistence, that contributed to his designs, and to their own destruction; whilst himself grew insensibly powerful enough to cut off those by whom he had climbed, in the instant that they projected to demolish their own building. What was said of Cinna may very justly be said of him, *ausum eum, quæ nemo auderet bonus; perfecisse, quæ à nullo, nisi fortissimo, perfici possent.*\* He attempted those things which no good man durst have ventured on; and atchieved those in which none but a valiant and great man could have succeeded. Without doubt, no man with more wickedness ever attempted any thing, or brought to pass what he desired more wickedly, more in the face and contempt of religion, and moral honesty; yet wickedness as great as his could never have accomplished those designs, without the assistance of a great spirit, an admirable circumspection, and sagacity, and a most magnanimous resolution.

When he appeared first in the parliament, he seemed to have a person in no degree gracious,† no ornament of discourse, none of those talents

---

\* Vell. Paterc, lib. 2. c. 24.

† *Sir Philip Warwick*, who yields to none of his contemporary historians in candour and integrity, gives a minute description of the deportment of Cromwell at this time. See *Warwick's memoirs of the reign of Charles I.* 8vo. p. 247.

which use to conciliate the affections of the stander by: yet as he grew into place and authority, his parts seemed to be raised, as if he had had concealed faculties, till he had occasion to use them: and when he was to act the part of a great man, he did it without any indecency, notwithstanding the want of custom.

After he was confirmed and invested protector, he consulted with very few upon any action of importance, nor communicated any enterprise he resolved upon, with more than those who were to have principal parts in the execution of it; nor with them sooner than was absolutely necessary. What he once resolved, in which he was not rash, he would not be dissuaded from, nor endure any contradiction of his power and authority; but extorted obedience from them who were not willing to yield it. He committed serjeant Maynard to the Tower for presuming (in Westminster-hall) to question or make doubt of his authority; and the judges were sent for, and severely reprehended for suffering that licence. Thus he subdued a spirit that had often been troublesome to the most sovereign power, and made Westminster-hall as obedient to his commands as any of the rest of his quarters. In all other matters which did not concern the life of his jurisdiction, he seemed to have great reverence for the law, rarely interposing between party and party. As he proceeded with this kind of indignation with those who were refractory, and durst contend with his greatness, so towards all who complied with his good pleasure, and courted his protection, he used great civility, generosity and bounty. To reduce three nations which perfectly hated him, to an entire obedience to all his dictates; to awe, and govern those nations by an army that was indevoted to him, and wished his ruin, was an instance of a very prodigious address. But his greatness at home, was but a shadow of the glory he had abroad. It was hard to discover, which feared him most, France, Spain, or the low countries, where his friendship was current at the value he put upon it. As they did all sacrifice their honour, and their interest, to his pleasure, so their is nothing he could have demanded, that either of them would have denied him.

To conclude his character, Cromwell was not so far a man of blood, as to follow Machiavel's method; which prescribes, upon a total alteration of government, as a thing absolutely necessary, to cut off all the heads of those, and extirpate their families, who are friends to the old one. It was confidently reported, that, in the council of officers, it was more than once proposed, "that there might be a general massacre of all the royal party, as the only expedient to secure the government," but that Cromwell would never consent to, it may be, out of too great a contempt of his enemies. In a word, as he was guilty of many crimes against which damnation is denounced, and for which hell-fire is prepared, so he had some good qualities which have caused the memory of some men in all ages to be celebrated; and he will be looked upon by posterity as a brave wicked man. III. 648.

---

GEORGE MONK, CR. DUKE OF ALBEMARLE, &c.
DIED MDCLXIX.

HE was of an ancient family in Devonshire, always very loyally affected, and being a younger brother, he entered early into the life and condition of a soldier. When the troubles began in Scotland, he betook himself to the service of the king, and was soon after sent into Ireland, where he served with singular reputation of courage and conduct.

He was taken prisoner at Namptwich, and remained in the Tower to the end of the war, when Cromwell prevailed upon him to engage himself again in the war of Ireland, and from that time he continued very firm to Cromwell, who was liberal and bountiful to him, and took him into his entire confidence.

After the death of Cromwell, Monk was looked upon as a man more inclined to the king, than any other in great authority, if he might discover it without too much loss or hazard. He had no fumes of fanaticism to turn his head, nor any credit with, or dependance upon any who were swayed by these trances.* III. 699.

* The reader must have recourse to the history itself for an account of this illustrious restorer of monarchy.

## EDWARD MONTAGU, CR. EARL OF SANDWICH, &c. LOST HIS LIFE IN THE BATTLE OF SOUTHWOLD BAY, MDCLXXII.

HE was of a noble family, of which some were too much addicted to innovations in religion, and in the beginning of the troubles he appeared against the king; though his father, who had been long a servant to the crown, never could be prevailed upon to swerve from his allegiance, and took all the care he could to restrain this his only son within those limits: but being young, and more out of his father's control by being married into a family,* which at that time, also trod awry, he was so far wrought upon by the caresses of Cromwell, that, out of pure affection to him, he was persuaded to take command in the army, when it was new modelled under Fairfax, and when he was little more than twenty years of age. He served in that army in the condition of a colonel to the end of the war, with the reputation of a very stout and sober young man. And from that

* Jemima, daughter of John Lord Crewe, of Stene.

time Cromwell, to whom he passionately adhered, took him into his nearest confidence, and sent him, first joined in commission with Blake; and then, in the sole command by sea; in which he was discreet and successful. And though men looked upon him as devoted to Cromwell's interest, in all other respects he behaved himself with civility to all men, and without the least shew of acrimony towards any who had served the king; and was so much in love with monarchy, that he was one of those who most desired and advised Cromwell to accept, and assume that title, when it was offered to him by his parliament.

He was of so excellent a temper and behaviour, that he could make himself no enemies; and of so many good qualities and so easy to live with, that he marvellously reconciled the minds of all men to him, who had not intimacy enough with him to admire his other parts, yet was in the general inclinations of men upon some disadvantage. They who had constantly followed the king, whilst he as constantly adhered to Cromwell, and knew not how early he had entertained repentance, and with what hazards and dangers he had manifested it, did believe the king had been too prodigal in heaping so many honours upon him. And they who had been familiar with him and of the same party, and thought they had been as active as he in contributing to the revolution, considered him with some anger, as one who had better luck than they, without more merit, and who had made early conditions; when in truth no man in the kingdom had been less guilty of that address; nor did he ever contribute to any advancement to which he arrived, by the least intimation or insinuation that he wished it, or that it would be acceptable to him. III. 729. Life III. 575.

---

## ARCHIBALD CAMPBELL, MARQUIS OF ARGYLE,— EXECUTED MDCLXI.

He was a man like *Drances*, in *Virgil*,
*Largus opum, et linguá melior, sed frigida bello
Dextera, consiliis habitus non futilis auctor,
Seditione potens.*

He was a person of extraordinary cunning, well bred, and though he did not appear with any great advantage at first sight, yet he reconciled even those who had aversion to him very strongly by a little conversation; insomuch as after so many repeated indignities (to say no worse) which he had put upon Charles I. and when he had continued the same affronts to his son, by hindering the Scots from inviting him, yet when he was landed, no man paid him so much reverence and outward respect, and gave so good an example to all others, with what veneration their king ought to be treated, as the marquis of Argyle did, and in a very short time made himself agreeable and acceptable to him.

His wit was pregnant, and his humour gay and pleasant, except when he liked not the company or the argument. When the opposite faction prevailed, in which there were likewise crafty managers, and that his counsels were commonly rejected, he carried himself so, that they who hated him most, were willing to compound with him, and that his majesty should not withdraw his countenance from him. Life II. 98.

### SIR RICHARD BROWNE——DIED MDCLXXXII.

HE was lord mayor of London (1661) a very stout and vigilant magistrate, who was equally feared and hated by all the seditious party, for his extraordinary zeal and resolution in the king's service. Nor was there any man in England who did raze out the memory of what he had formerly done amiss, with a more signal acknowledgment, or a more frank and generous engagement against all manner of factions, which opposed or obstructed his majesty's service; which made him terrible and odious to all, and to none more than to the presbyterians who had seduced him.* (During his mayoralty he quelled Venner's conspiracy with singular courage and activity.) Life, II. 136.

* He had been a major-general of the parliament army. In 1648, Sir Richard Browne, Sir John Clotworthy, Sir William Waller, major-general Massey and commissary-general Copley were the most active members in the house, of the presbyterian party. III. 240.

## JOHN, SECOND LORD ROBERTS, CR. EARL OF RADNOR——DIED MDCLXXXV.

THOUGH of a good understanding, he was of so morose a nature, that it was no easy matter to treat with him. He had some pedantic parts of learning, which made his other parts of judgment the worse. He was naturally proud and imperious, which humour was encreased by an ill education; for excepting some years spent in the inns of court, he might be very justly said to have been born and bred in Cornwall. When Lord Deputy in Ireland, he received the information of the chief persons there so negligently, and gave his answers so scornfully, that they besought the king that they might not be obliged to attend him any more; but he was not a man that was to be disgraced and thrown off without much inconvenience and hazard. He had parts which in council and parliament were very troublesome, for of all men alive who had so few friends, he had the most followers. They who conversed most with him, knew him to have many humours which were very intolerable; they who were but little acquainted with him, took him to be a man of much knowledge, and called his morosity gravity. Life II. 193.

---

SIR HENRY BENNET, CR. EARL OF ARLINGTON,—
DIED MDCLXXXV.

HE was a man unversed in any business, who never had, nor ever was like to speak in the house, except in his ear who sat next him, to the disadvantage of some who had spoken, and had not the faculties to get himself beloved, and was thought by all men to be a roman catholic; for which they had not any other reason but from his indifference in all things which concerned the church. Life II. 356.

## SIR WILLIAM MORRICE, KNT.——DIED MDCLXVIII.

HE was preferred to the office of secretary of state purely to gratify and oblige general Monk, whose friend and kinsman he was. He had a good reputation in the house of commons, and did the business of his office without reproach. He had lived most part of his time in the country, with the repute of a wise man and a very good scholar; but being without any knowledge in the modern languages, he gave the king often occasion to laugh at his unskilful pronunciation of many words. In the latin dispatches, which concern all the northern parts, he was ready, and treated with those ambassadors fluently and elegantly; and for all domestic affairs no man doubted his sufficiency, except in the garb and mode, and humour of the court. Life II. 368.

## SIR GEORGE DOWNING, KNT. AND BART.—DIED ABOUT MDCLXX.

HE was of an obscure birth, and a more obscure education, which he had received in New England; he had passed through many offices in Cromwell's army, and at last got a very particular credit and confidence with him, and under that countenance married a beautiful lady of a very noble extraction, which was the fate of many bold men in that presumptious time. And when Cromwell had subdued the Dutch, he sent this man to reside as his agent with them, being a man of a proud and insolent spirit, and who would add to any imperious command of his somewhat of the bitterness of his own spirit. He contrived however to continue resident in Holland after the restoration of the king. Life II. 343.

---

## SIR JOHN LAWSON, KNT.——DIED MDCLXV.

HE had such eminent skill and conduct in all maritime occasions, that his counsel was most considered in all debates, and the greatest seamen were ready to receive advice from him. He was of Yorkshire, near Scarborough, and of that rank of people who are bred to the sea from their cradle. His industry and sobriety made him quickly taken notice of, and to be preferred from a common sailor to the command of the best ships.

He was in all the actions performed by Blake, and in all the battles which Cromwell fought with the Dutch. He served Charles II. with equal fidelity, and performed to his death all that could be expected from a brave and an honest man. Life II. 508.

---

SIR RICHARD FANSHAWE, KNT. AND BART.——
DIED MDCLXVI.

HE was a gentleman very well known and very well beloved; had been first ambassador in Portugal, and had behaved himself so well there, that when he returned from thence he was recommended, and upon the matter desired, by that crown to be sent to Spain, as the fittest person to mediate in the king's name between Spain and Portugal; and the king had before designed to send him ambassador into spain to settle a treaty between that country and England. No man knew that court better, or was so well versed in the language, having lived there many years in much better times. He had remained there about two years with such frequent mortifications as ministers use to meet with in courts irresolute and perplexed in their own affairs, and had made a journey to Lisbon upon the earnest desire of Spain, and returned without effect. On a sudden a project for a treaty was sent him, containing more advantages in trade to the nation (which are the most important matters in all those treaties) and insisting upon fewer inconvenient conditions, than had ever been in any of the former; which treaty, with some secret article respecting Portugal, he presently signed, and sent to England, where many faults were found with it; for besides Sir Richard's absence, who would with greater abilities have defended himself, than any of those who reproached him, it was no advantage to him that he was known to be much in Lord Clarendon's confidence. In the end the king concluded that he would not sign the treaty, and the ambassador was recalled, and died at Madrid on the point of setting out for England.* Life III. 582.

---

SIR NICHOLAS HYDE, LORD CHIEF JUSTICE OF ENGLAND, UNCLE TO LORD CLARENDON,—— DIED MDCXXXI.

HE was a man of excellent learning for that province he was to govern, of unsuspected and unblemished integrity, of an exemplary gravity

* He had a promise to be secretary of state, in which he was disappointed; and was afterwards recalled from his embassy to make way for the earl of Sandwich. The memoirs of Sir Richard Fanshawe, and the sufferings of his family for the crown, exquisitely written by his wife (one of the daughters of Sir John Harrison, of Balls, Knt.) who with her sister Margaret (married to Sir Edm. Turnor of Stoke-Rochford, co. Lincoln, Knt.) were the constant attendants of Sir Richard throughout the civil war, are in the possession of the family, and might, from the interesting matter they contain, prove an acceptable present to the public. *See the European Magazine for 1798.*

and austerity, which was necessary for the manners of that time, corrupted by the marching of armies, and by the licence after the disbanding them; and though upon his promotion some years before (1626) from a private practicer of the law, to the supreme judicatory in it, by the power and recommendation of the great favorite, of whose counsel he had been, he was exposed to much envy and some prejudice; yet his behaviour was so grateful to all the judges, who had an entire confidence in him, his service so useful to the king in his government, his justice and sincerity so conspicuous throughout the kingdom, that the death of no judge had at any time been more lamented. He died of a malignant fever, gotten from the infection of some gaol in his summer circuit. Life I. 11.

---

#### HENRY HYDE, FATHER TO LORD CLARENDON——DIED MDCXXXII.

HE wanted about six weeks of attaining the age of seventy, and was the greatest instance of the felicity of a country life that was seen in that age; having enjoyed a competent, and to him a plentyful fortune, a very great réputation of piety and virtue, and his death being attended with universal lamentation. It cannot be expressed with what agony his son bore his loss, having, as he was used to say, "not only lost the best father, but the best friend, and the best companion he ever had or could have;" and he was never so well pleased, as when he had fit occasions given him to mention his father, whom he did in truth believe to be the wisest man he had ever known; and he was often heard to say in the time when his condition was at the highest, " that though God Almighty had been very propitious to him, in raising him to great honours and preferments, he did not value any honour he had so much as the being the son of such a father and mother, for whose sakes principally he thought God had conferred those blessings upon him." Life I. 18.

## BEN JONSON——DIED MDCXXXVII.

HIS name can never be forgotten, having by his very good learning, and the severity of his nature and manners very much reformed the stage, and indeed the English poetry itself. His natural advantages were, judgment to order and govern fancy, rather than excess of fancy, his productions being slow and upon deliberation, yet then abounding with great wit and fancy, and will live accordingly; and surely as he did exceedingly exalt the English language in eloquence, propriety, and masculine expressions; so he was the best judge of and fittest to prescribe rules to poetry and poets, of any man who had lived with, or before him, or since; if Mr. Cowley had not made a flight beyond all men, with that modesty yet, to ascribe much of this, to the example and learning of Ben Jonson. Life I. 30.

### JOHN SELDEN——DIED MDCLIV.

HE was a person whom no character can flatter, or transmit in any expressions equal to his merit and virtue, he was of so stupendous a learning in all kinds, and in all languages (as may appear in his excellent and transcendant writings) that a man would have thought he had been entirely conversant amongst books, and had never spent an hour but in reading and writing; yet his humanity, courtesy, and affability were such, that he would have been thought to have been bred in the best courts, but that his good nature, charity, and delight in doing good exceeded that breeding. His style in all his writings seems harsh and sometimes obscure; which is not wholly to be imputed to the abstruse subjects of which he commonly treated, out of the paths trod by other men; but to a little undervaluing the beauty of style, and too much propensity to the language of antiquity; but in his conversation he was the most clear discourser, and had the best faculty in making hard things easy, and presenting them to the understanding, of any man that hath been known. If he had some infirmities with other men, they were weighed down with wonderful and prodigious abilities and excellencies in the other scale. Life I. 31.

---

### CHARLES COTTON——DIED MDCLXXXVII.

HE was a gentleman born to a competent fortune, and so qualified in his person and education, that for many years he continued the greatest ornament of the town, in the esteem of those who had been best bred. His natural parts were very great, his wit flowing in all the parts of conversation; the superstructure of learning not raised to a considerable height; but having passed some years in Cambridge, and then in France, and conversing always with learned men, his expressions were ever proper and significant, and gave great lustre to his discourse, upon any argument; so that he was thought by those who were not intimate with him, to have been much better acquainted with books than he was. He had all those qualities which in youth raise men to the reputation of being fine gentlemen; such a pleasantness and gaiety of humour, such a sweetness and gentleness of nature, and such a civility and delightfulness in conversation, that no man in the court or out of it, appeared a more accomplished person; all these extraordinary qualifications being supported by as extraordinary a clearness of courage, and fearlessness of spirit, of which he gave too often manifestation. Life I. 32.

---

### SIR JOHN VAUGHAN———DIED MDCLXXIV.

WHEN a student of the Inner Temple, he indulged more in the politer learning; and was in truth a man of great parts of nature, and very well adorned by arts and books, and so much cherished by Mr. Selden, that he grew to be of entire truth and friendship with him, and to that owed the best part of his reputation; for he was of so magisterial and supercilious a humour, so proud and insolent a behaviour, that all Mr. Selden's instructions, and authority and example, could not file off that roughness of his nature, so as to make him very grateful. He looked most into those parts of the law, which disposed him to least reverence to the crown, and most to popular authority; yet without inclination to any change in government; and therefore before the beginning of the civil war, and when he clearly discerned the approaches to it in parliament (of which he was a member) he withdrew himself into the fastnesses of his own country, North Wales, where he enjoyed a secure, and as near an innocent life, as the iniquity of that time would permit; and upon the return of king Charles the second, he appeared under the character of a man, who had preserved his loyalty entire, and was esteemed accordingly by all that party.

His friend Mr. Hyde, who was then become lord high chancellor of England, renewed his old kindness and friendship towards him, and was desirous to gratify him all the ways he could, and earnestly pressed him to put on his gown again, and take upon him the office of a judge; but he excused himself upon his long discontinuance (having not worn his gown, and wholly discontinued the profession from the year 1640, full twenty years) and upon his age, and expressly refused to receive any promotion; but continued all the professions of respect and gratitude imaginable to the chancellor, till it was in his power to manifest the contrary, to his prejudice, which he did with circumstances very uncommendable.\* Life I. 32.

---

### SIR KENHELM DIGBY——DIED MDCLXV.

HE was a person very eminent and notorious throughout the whole course of his life, from his cradle to his grave; of an ancient family and noble extraction, and inherited a fair and plentiful fortune, notwithstanding the attainder of his father. He was a man of a very extraordinary person and presence, which drew the eyes of all men upon him, which were more fixed by a wonderful graceful behaviour, a flowing courtesy and civility, and such a volubility of language, as sur-

\* He was made chief justice of the common pleas, 1668.—*his portrait is in Guildhall.*

prized and delighted; and though in another man it might have appeared to have somewhat of affectation, it was marvellously graceful in him, and seemed natural to his size, the mould of his person, to the gravity of his motion and the tune of his voice and delivery. He had a fair reputation in arms, of which he gave an early testimony in his youth, in some encounters in Spain, and Italy, and afterwards in an action in the Mediterranean. In a word, he had all the advantages that nature, and art, and an excellent education could give him; which, with a great confidence and presence of mind, buoyed him up against all those prejudices and disadvantages, which would have suppressed and sunk any other man, but never clouded or eclipsed him, from appearing in the best places, and the best company, and with the best estimation and satisfaction. Life I. 33.

### THOMAS MAY——DIED MDCL.

HE was the eldest son of his father, a knight, and born to a fortune, if his father had not spent it; so that he had only an annuity left him, not proportionable to a liberal education; yet since his fortune could not raise his mind, he brought his mind down to his fortune, by a great modesty and humility in his nature, which was not affected, but very well became an imperfection in his speech, which was a great mortification to him, and kept him from entering into any discourse, but in the company of his very friends. His parts of nature and art were very good, as appears by his translation of Lucan (none of the easiest work of that kind) and more by his supplement to Lucan, which being entirely his own, for the learning, the wit and the language, may be well looked upon as one of the best epic poems in the English language. Upon his majesty's refusal to give him a small pension, he prostituted himself to the vile office of celebrating the infamous acts of those who were in rebellion against the king; which he did so meanly, that he seemed to all men to have lost his wits when he left his honesty. Life I. 35.

### THOMAS CAREW——DIED ABOUT MDCXXXIX.

HE was a younger brother of a good family, and of excellent parts, and had spent many years of his youth in France and Italy, and returning from travel, followed the court; which the modesty of that time disposed men to do some time, before they pretended to be of it; and he was very much esteemed by the most eminent persons in the court, and well looked upon by the king himself. He was a person of a pleasant and facetious wit, and made many poems, (especially in the amorous way) which for the sharpness of the fancy, and the elegancy of the language, in which that fancy was spread, were at least equal, if not superior to any of that time: but his glory was, that after fifty years of his life, spent with less severity and exactness than it ought to have been, he died with the greatest remorse for that licence, and with the greatest manifestation of christianity, that his best friends could desire. Life* I. 36.

* Lord Clarendon was often heard to say, "that if he had any thing good in him, in his humour, or in his manners, he owed it to the example, and the information he had received

### SIR FRANCIS WENMAN—DIED ABOUT MDCXLII.

HE was of a noble extraction, and of an ancient family in Oxfordshire, where he was possessed of a competent estate; but his reputation of wisdom and integrity gave him an interest and credit in that country, much above his fortune; and no man had more esteem in it, or power over it. He was a neighbour to the Lord Falkland, and in so entire friendship and confidence with him, that he had great authority in the society of all his friends and acquaintance. He was a man of great sharpness of understanding, and of a piercing judgment; no man better understood the affections and temper of the kingdom, or indeed the nature of the nation, or discerned farther the consequence of counsels, and with what success they were like to be attended. He was a very good latin scholar, but his ratiocination was above his learning; and the sharpness of his wit incomparable. He was equal to the greatest trust and employment, if

in, and from that company, with most of whom he had an entire friendship," namely, Lord Falkland before-mentioned, and the following characters. Life I. 37.

he had been ambitious of it, or solicitous for it; but his want of health produced a kind of laziness of mind, which disinclined him to business. He died before the general troubles of the kingdom, which he foresaw with wonderful concern, and when many wise men were weary of living so long. Life I. 45.

### SIDNEY GODOLPHIN——SLAIN AT CHAGFORD, MDCXLII.

HE was a younger brother of Sir F. Godolphin, but by the provision left by his father, and by the death of a younger brother, he was liberally supplied for a very good education, and for a cheerful subsistence, in any course of life he proposed to himself. There was never so great a mind and spirit contained in so little room; so large an understanding, and so unrestrained a fancy, in so very small a body; so that the Lord Falkland used to say merrily, that he thought it was a great ingredient in his friendship for Mr. Godolphin, that he was pleased to be found in his company, where he was the properer man; and it may be, the very remarkableness of his little person made the sharpness of his wit, and the composed quickness of his judgment and understanding, the more notable. He had spent some years in France, and in the low countries; and accompanied the Earl of Leicester in his ambassage into Denmark, before he resolved to be quiet, and attend some promotion in the court; where his excellent disposition and manners, and extraordinary qualifications, made him very acceptable. Though every body loved his company very well, yet he loved very much to be alone, being in his constitution inclined somewhat to melancholy, and to retirement amongst his books; and was so far from being active, that he was contented to be reproached by his friends with laziness; and was of so nice and tender a composition, that a little rain or wind would disorder him, and divert him from any short journey, he had most willingly proposed to himself. Yet the civil war no sooner began (the first approaches towards which he discovered as soon as any man, by the proceedings in parliament, where he was a member, and opposed with great indignation) than he put himself into the first troops which were raised in the west for the king; and bore the uneasiness and fatigue of winter marches with an exemplary courage and alacrity; until by too brave a pursuit of the enemy, into an obscure village in Devonshire, he was shot with a musket; with which (without saying any word more, than " O God, I am hurt") he fell dead from his horse; to the excessive grief of his friends, who were all that knew him; and the irreparable damage of the public. Life I. 46.

---

EDMUND WALLER——DIED MDCLXXXVII.

HE was born to a very fair estate, by the parsimony, or frugality, of a wise father and mother; and he thought it so commendable an advantage, that he resolved to improve it with his utmost care, upon which, in his nature, he was too much intent; and in order to that, he was so much reserved and retired, that he was scarce ever heard of, till, by his address and dexterity, he had gotten a very rich wife in the city, against all the recommendation and countenance of the court, which was thoroughly engaged on the behalf of Mr. Crofts; and which used to be successful, in that age, against any opposition. He had the good fortune to have an alliance and friendship with Dr. Morley, who had assisted and instructed him in the reading many good books, to which his natural parts and promptitude inclined him; especially the poets. At the age when other men used to give over writing verses (for he was near thirty years of age, when he first engaged himself in that exercise, at least, that he was known to do so) he surprised the town with two or three pieces of that kind; as if a tenth muse had been newly born to cherish drooping poetry. The Doctor, at that time, brought him into that company which was most celebrated for good conversation; where he was received and esteemed with great applause and respect. He was a very pleasant discourser in earnest and in jest, and therefore very grateful to all kind of company, where he was not the less esteemed for being very rich.

He had been even nursed in parliaments, where he sat when he was very young; and so, when they were resumed again (after a long intermission) he appeared in those assemblies with great advantage;

having a graceful way of speaking, and by thinking much upon several arguments (which his temper and complexion, that had much of melancholic, inclined him to) he seemed often to speak upon the sudden, when the occasion had only administered the opportunity of saying what he had thoroughly considered, which gave a great lustre to all he said; which was yet rather of delight than weight. There needs no more be said to extol the excellence and power of his wit, and pleasantness of his conversation, than that it was of magnitude enough to cover a world of very great faults; that is, so to cover them, that they were not taken notice of to his reproach; namely, a narrowness in his nature to the lowest degree; an abjectness and want of courage to support him in any virtuous undertaking; an insinuation, and servile flattery to the height the vainest and most imperious nature could be contented with: his company was acceptable where his spirit was odious; and he was at least pitied, where he was most detested. Life I. 47.

#### GILBERT SHELDON, ARCHBISHOP OF CANTERBURY.
#### DIED MDCLXXVII.

HIS learning, gravity, and prudence, had raised him to such a reputation, when he was domestic chaplain to the Lord Keeper Coventry, (who exceedingly esteemed him, and used his service not only in all matters relating to the church, but in many other businesses of importance, in which that great and good Lord was nearly concerned) and when he was afterwards warden of All-Souls college in Oxford, that he was looked upon as very equal to any preferment the church could yield. And Sir Francis Wenman would often say, when the doctor resorted to the conversation at Lord Falkland's house as he frequently did, that " Dr. Sheldon was born and bred to be archbishop of Canterbury." Life I. p. 49.

---

#### GEORGE MORLEY, BISHOP OF WINCHESTER
#### ——DIED MDCLXXXIV.

HE was a gentleman of very eminent parts in all polite learning; of great wit and readiness, and

subtilty in disputation; and of remarkable temper and prudence in conversation, which rendered him most grateful in all the best company. He was then chaplain in the house, and to the family of Lord Carnarvon, which then needed a wise and a wary director. From some academic contests he had been engaged in, during his living in Christ Church in Oxford, where he was always of the first eminency, he had by the natural faction and animosity of those disputes fallen under the reproach of holding some opinions, which were not then grateful to those churchmen, who had the greatest power in ecclesiastical promotions; and some sharp answers and replies he used to make in accidental discourses, and which in truth, were made for mirth and pleasantness sake (as he was of the highest facetiousness), were reported and spread abroad, to his prejudice: as being once asked by a grave country gentleman (who was desirous to be instructed what their tenets and opinions were) "what the Arminians held?" He pleasantly answered, " that they held all the best bishopricks and deaneries in England," which was quickly reported abroad, as Dr. Morley's definition of the arminian tenets. He was a person above all possible reproach, and was known and valued by more persons of honour than most of the clergy were, being not only without the envy of any preferment; but under the advantage of a discountenanced person. Life I. 49.

---

### JOHN EARL, D. D. BISHOP OF SALISBURY——DIED MDCLXIII.

HE was a person very notable for his elegance in the Greek and Latin tongues, and having been fellow of Merton college in Oxford, and having been proctor of the university, and some very witty and sharp discourses being published in print without his consent, though known to be his, he grew suddenly into a very general esteem with all men; being a man of great piety and devotion; a most eloquent and powerful preacher; and of a conversation so pleasant and delightful, so very innocent, and so very facetious, that no man's company was more desired and more loved. No man was more negligent in his dress, and habit and mien; no man more wary and cultivated in his behaviour and discourse; insomuch as he had the greater advantage when he was known, by promising so little before he was known. He was an excellent poet both in Latin, Greek and English, as appears by many pieces yet abroad; though he suppressed many more himself, especially English, incomparably good, out of an austerity to those sallies of his youth. He was very dear to the lord Falkland, with whom he spent as much time, as he could make his own; and as that lord would impute the speedy progress he made in the Greek tongue to the information and assistance he had from Mr. Earl, so Mr. Earl would frequently profess, that he had got more useful learning by his conversation at Tew (the lord Falkland's house) than he had at Oxford. He was amongst the few excellent men who never had, nor ever could have an enemy; but such an one who was an enemy to all learning and virtue, and therefore would never make himself known. Life I. 51.

## JOHN HALES, OF ETON.——DIED MDCLVI.

HE had been Greek professor in the university of Oxford; and had borne the greatest part of the labour of that excellent edition of St. Chrysostom's works, set out by sir Harry Saville; who was then warden of Merton college, when the other was fellow of that house. He was chaplain in the house with sir Dudley Carleton, ambassadour at the Hague, at the time when the synod of Dort was held, and so had liberty to be present at the consultations in that assembly; and hath left the best memorial behind him of the ignorance, passion, animosity, and injustice of that convention; of which he often made very pleasant relations; though at that time it received too much countenance from England. He would never take any cure of souls; and was so great a contemner of money, that he was wont to say, that his fellowship, and the bursar's place (which for the good of the college he held many years) was worth fifty pounds a year more than he could spend; and yet, beside his being very charitable to all poor people, even to liberality; he had made a greater and better collection of books than were to be found in any other private library that I have seen. He had read more, and carried more about him, in his excellent memory, than any man I ever knew, my lord Falkland only excepted. He would often say, that he would renounce the church of England to-morrow, if it obliged him to believe that any other christians should be damned; and that nobody would conclude another man to be damned who did not wish him so. No man more strict and severe to himself, to other men so charitable as to their opinions, that he thought other men were more in fault for their carriage towards them, than the men themselves were who erred; and he thought that pride and passion, more than conscience, were the cause of all separation from each others communion; and he frequently said that that only kept the world from agreeing upon such a liturgy, as might bring them into one communion, all doctrinal points upon which men differed in their opinions, being to have no place in any liturgy. He was one of the least men in the kingdom, and one of the greatest scholars in Europe.* — Life I. 53.

* He was called the ever-memorable Hales.

## WILLIAM CHILLINGWORTH——DIED MDCXLIV.

HE was of a stature little superior to Mr. Hales (and it was an age in which there were many great and wonderful men of that size) and a man of so great a subtilty of understanding, and so rare a temper in debate, that as it was impossible to provoke him into any passion, so it was very difficult to keep a man's self from being a little discomposed by his sharpness and quickness of argument.

He had with his notable perfection in disputation, contracted such an irresolution and habit of doubting, as made him reconcile himself too soon to the church of Rome, and having made a journey to St. Omers, purely to perfect his conversion, he found as little satisfaction there, and returned with as much haste from them, with a belief that an "entire exemption from error was neither inherent in, nor necessary to any church:" which occasioned that war which was carried on by the Jesuits with so great asperity and reproaches against him, and in which he defended himself by such an admirable eloquence of language, and clear and incomparable power of reason, that he not only made them appear unequal adversaries, but carried the war into their own quarters; and made the Pope's infallibility to be as much shaken, and declined by their own doctors, and to be at least as much doubted, as in the schools of the reformed or protestant church. Neither the books of the adversary, nor any of their persons, though he was acquainted with the best of both, had ever made great impression upon him; all his doubts grew out of himself, when he assisted his scruples with all the strength of his own reason; so that he was in truth in all his sallies and retreats his own convert.

He was a man of excellent parts, and of a cheerful disposition, void of all kind of vice, and endued with many notable virtues; of a very public heart, and an indefatigable desire to do good; his only unhappiness proceeded from his sleeping too little, and thinking too much, which sometimes threw him into violent fevers.* Life I. 55.

* He was taken prisoner by Sir W. Waller at Arundel Castle, where he died from the barbarous usage he met with, to the grief of all who knew *him*, or his famous work, the *Religion of Protestants a safe way to salvation*.

### EDWARD HYDE, CR. EARL OF CLARENDON.
#### DIED MDCLXXIV.

HE was of a very cheerful and open nature, without any dissimulation, and delivered his opinion of things or persons, where it was convenient, without reserve or disguise; and was at least tenacious enough of his opinion, and never departed from it out of compliance with any man. Though he was of a complexion and humour very far from despair; yet he did believe the king would be oppressed by the party which then (1642) governed; and that they who followed and served him would be destroyed; so that it was not ambition of power, or wealth, that engaged him to embark in so very hazardous an employment; but abstractedly the consideration of his duty; and he often used to apply those words of Cicero to himself, *mea ætas incidit in id bellum, cujus altera pars sceleris nimium habuit, altera felicitatis parum.* Life I. 96.

* It appears from the memoirs of his own life (to which the reader must be referred) that he had all the virtue of a Cato; and it is no less evident that he had something of his roughness and severity. *Granger.* IV. 64.

Harding sculpt

# LORD CLARANDON

Pub 1 Nov 1794 by I Herbert 29 Russell St Blo...

### EPITAPH IN WESTMINSTER ABBEY.

"Edward Earl of Clarendon, Lord Chancellor of England, the most excellent historian of the late times, who for his firm religion, unshaken loyalty, sincere love of his country, unbiassed integrity, and universal humanity and munificence, was (after serving the martyred father in his affliction, conducting the exiled son and restoring him, preserving his country's privileges after the restoration, and mitigating the just displeasure of the king against the rebels) by that very prince he had served, that country he had preserved, and those factions he had with lenity endeavoured to moderate, rewarded with banishment in his old age. He died of the gout at Rouen in Normandy." *Dart's History of Westminster Abbey, II. 61. (There are no traces of this inscription left; it is said to have been in the area near the chapel of St. Andrew.)*

## THE END.

# INDEX.

The names of persons incidentally mentioned are in italics.

ABBOT, Abp. 47
Albemarle, D. of, 161. 170
Arundel, E. of, 30
*Arundels* 136
Argyle, M. of, 165. 143
Arlington, E. of 169
Astley, Lord, 131
*Archer,* } *Judges,* 134
*Atkyns,*
Aubigney, Lord, 97
Bastwick, J. 79
Bedford, E. of, 62. 64
Blake, Adm. 153. 164. 172
*Boswell, J.* 85
Bristol, G. E. of, 90. 128
Bristol, J. E. of, 105
Brentford, E. of, 127
*Bridgman,* } *Judges,* 134
*Brown,*
Browne, Sir R. 167
Brooke, Lord, 98. 99
Buckingham, D. of, 20. 17. 43. 77. 91. 113
*Buckhurst, Lord,* 37
Burton, H. 80
*Byron, Lord,* 87
Capel, Lord, 141
Cavendish, Sir C. 109
*Cæsar, Sir J.* 28
Carlisle, E. of, 38
*Clare, E. of,* 77
Carnarvon, E. of, 124. 193
Carew, Tho. 185

Chillingworth, W. 198
Charles I. 16. 144. 166
*Charles II.* 83. 102. 147. 149. 172
Chandos, Lord, 132
Clarendon, E. of, 200. 46. 102. 123. 173. 181. 185
*Clotworthy, Sir J.* 167
*Cowley, Mr.* 177.
Cotton, Ch. 179
Coventry, Ld. 23. 29. 54. 57. 82. 192
Coke, Sir J. 41. 42
Cottington, Lord 55, 51
Conway, Lord, 60
*Copley, Mr.* 61
——— *Com. Gen.* 167
Colepepper, Lord, 89. 128
*Crew, Lord,* 163
*Crofts, Mr.* 190
Cromwell, O. 157. 67. 118. 149. 150. 152. 153. 156. 162. 163. 164. 171
Derby, E. of, 147. 146
Digby, Sir K. 182
*Digby, Lord,* 90. 106. 128
Dorchester, Visc. 42. 196
Dorset, E. of, 37
Downing, Sir G. 171
Earl, Bp. 194
*Eliz. Queen.* 43
Essex, E. of, 68. 114. 141.
Fanshawe, Sir R. 172
*Fairfax, Gen.* 140. 148. 163

# INDEX.

*Falconbridge, Lord,* 156
Falkland, E. of, 84. 186. 187.
192. 195. 197
Fiennes, N. 75
Finch, Lord, 45. 82
Gage, Sir H. 135
Glanville, Serj. 58
Godolphin, S. 187
Goring, Lord, 128
Grandison, Visc. 122
Grenville, Sir B. 121
*Hale, Judge,* 134
Hales J. 196. 198
Hamilton, J. D. of, 57. 51.
Hamilton, W. D. of, 137
Hampden, J. 72. 74. 76. 86
Herbert, Sir Edw. 83
Hertford, M. of, 94. 110. 153.
155
*Harrison, Sir J.* 174
Hewitt, Dr. 156.
Holland, E of, 40. 114
Holles, Lord, 77
Hopton, Lord 131
*Hume,* 61. 90
Hyde, Sir N. 174
Hyde, H. 175
*Hyde, Edw.* 46
*James, King,* 38. 40. 43. 80.
92. 94. 101. 105. 115
*Johnson, Dr.* 85.
*Jersey, E. of,* 123
Jonson, Ben, 177
Ireton, Hen. 148. 140
*Kelyng, Judge,* 134
Killegrew, Sir H. 136
*Kimbolton, L.* 66
Laud, Archbp. 49. 48
Lauderdale, D. of, 138
Lawson, Sir J. 171
Leicester, E. of, 104. 188
*Lenox, D. of,* 27
Lenthall, Wm. 61
Lindsey, E. of, 95

Littleton, Lord, 81
Lilburn, J. 151
Lisle, Sir G. 139
Lucas, Sir C. 139
Manchester, H. E. of, 28
Manchester, E. Earl of, 65.
114
*Mandeville, Visc.* 28
*Massey, Major Gen.* 167
*Maynard, Serj.* 159
May, Tho. 183
Morley, Bp. 192. 190
Morrice, Sir W. 170
*Morrison, Sir C.* 141
Morton, Sir W. 133
Montrose, M. of, 143
Newcastle, D. of, 107. 145
*Neyl, Dr.* 80
Nicholas, Sir Edw. 112
Northampton, E. of, 99
Northumberland, E. of, 114.
118
*Norwich, E. of,* 128
Noy, W. 44. 46
*Ormond, M. of,* 146.
Pembroke, W. E. of, 33.
Pembroke, P. E. of, 35.
114
Pennyman, Sir W. 134
*Pennyman, Sir J.* 135
Portland, E. of, 25. 50
Prynne, W. 78
Pym, J. 70. 62
*Raynsford, Judge,* 134
Richmond, D. of, 101. 97
Radnor, E. of, 168
*Rochester, E. of,* 128
Rupert P. 128. 96. 153. 155
Salisbury, E. of, 115
Sandwich, E. of, 163. 174
Say and Sele, Lord, 63. 114
*Saville, Sir H.* 196
Selden, J. 178. 82. 180
Seymour, Lord, 110

# INDEX.

Scrope, Sir Ger. ⎫ 96
—— Sir Adr. ⎭
St. John, Oliv. 74
Shelden, Archbp. 192
Slanning, Sir N. 121
Slannings, 136
Slingsby, Sir H. 155
Smith, Sir J. 125
Stuart, Lord J. 125. 97
Stuart, Lord B. 97
Stafford, E. of, 52. 50. 78. 95. 103. 105. 111. 120
Somerset, E. of, 33
Southampton, E. of, 102
Sussex, E. of, 111
Tiddesley, Sir T. 146
Topham, J. 60
Torrington, E. of, 83
Trelawnies, ⎫ 136
Trevanions, ⎭
Twisden, ⎫
Tyrrell, ⎬ Judges, 134
Turnor, ⎭

Tullibardine, E. of, 28
Turnor, Sir Edm. 174.
Vane, Sir Hen. sen. 119. 52. 54
Vane, Sir H. jun. 76
Vere, Lord, 60
Vaughan, Sir J. 180
Villiers, Edw. 123
Waller, Edm. 189
Waller Sir W., 133. 167. 199
Warwick, E. of, 117. 40
Warwick, Sir P. 158.
Wenman, Sir F. 186. 192
Williams, Archbp. 92
Windebank, Sec. 113
Wilmot, Visc. 128
Windham, Judge, 134
Widdrington, Lord, 144
Wildman, J. 150
Zouch, Lord, 112

From the Press of
*W. BULMER & CO.*

Just published, by R. Faulder, in one volume 4to. A Catalogue of engraved British Portraits from Egbert the great to the present time, with biographical notices. By Henry Bromley.

## L<sup>d</sup> Kingston

Vandyke pinx.  W. I. Taylor sc.

*Archbishop Juxon*

Publish'd March 1st 1794 by I. Her...

L<sup>d</sup> LITCHFIELD

C PENRUDDOCK

Pub 1 Jun 1794

www.ingramcontent.com/pod-product-compliance
Lightning Source LLC
Chambersburg PA
CBHW021811230426
43669CB00008B/710